ASSAULT
ON JUNO

ASSAULT
ON JUNO

MARK ZUEHLKE

RAVEN BOOKS
an imprint of
ORCA BOOK PUBLISHERS

Library and Archives Canada Cataloguing in Publication

Zuehlke, Mark
Assault on Juno / Mark Zuehlke.
(Rapid reads)

Issued also in electronic formats.
ISBN 978-1-4598-0036-6

1. World War, 1939-1945--Campaigns--France--Normandy.
2. Canada. Canadian Army--History--World War, 1939-1945.
3. Readers (Adult). 4. High interest-low vocabulary books.
I. Title. II. Series: Rapid reads
D756.5.N6Z823 2012   940.54'21421   C2011-907750-7

First published in the United States, 2012
Library of Congress Control Number: 2011943698

Summary: A dramatic account of the Canadian Forces attack on
Juno Beach on D-Day, June 6, 1944—a battle that began the march
toward victory in World War II.

*Orca Book Publishers is dedicated to preserving the environment and has
printed this book on paper certified by the Forest Stewardship Council®.*

Orca Book Publishers gratefully acknowledges the support for
its publishing programs provided by the following agencies:
the Government of Canada through the Canada Book Fund and the
Canada Council for the Arts, and the Province of British Columbia through
the BC Arts Council and the Book Publishing Tax Credit.

Design by Teresa Bubela
Cover image by Getty Images (Hulton Archive / Stringer)
Maps by Stuart Daniel, Starshell Maps

ORCA BOOK PUBLISHERS
PO Box 5626, Stn. B
Victoria, BC Canada
V8R 6S4

ORCA BOOK PUBLISHERS
PO Box 468
Custer, WA USA
98240-0468

www.orcabook.com
Printed and bound in Canada.

15 14 13 12 • 4 3 2 1

In memory of my father,
Charles Walter Zuehlke (1920–2011).

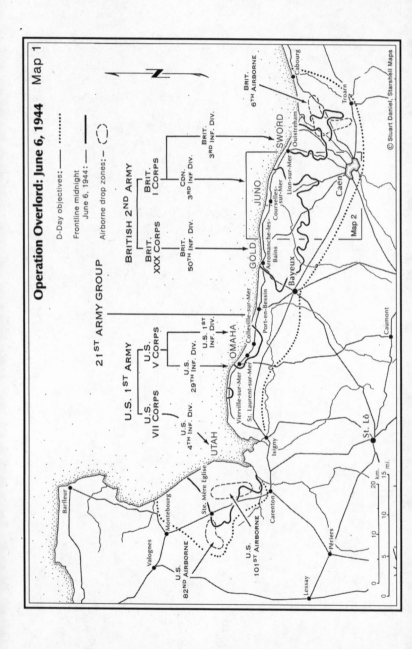

Operation Overlord: June 6, 1944   Map 1

D-Day objectives: ••••••••
Frontline midnight
June 6, 1944: ━━━
Airborne drop zones: ⌇

© Stuart Daniel, Starshell Maps

21ST ARMY GROUP

U.S. 1ST ARMY

U.S. VII CORPS
4TH INF. DIV.

U.S. V CORPS
U.S. 29TH INF. DIV.
U.S. 1ST INF. DIV.

BRITISH 2ND ARMY

BRIT. XXX CORPS
BRIT. 50TH INF. DIV.

BRIT. I CORPS
CDN. 3RD INF. DIV.
BRIT. 3RD INF. DIV.

BRIT. 6TH AIRBORNE

UTAH
OMAHA
GOLD
JUNO
SWORD

U.S. 82ND AIRBORNE
U.S. 101ST AIRBORNE

Barfleur
Valognes
Montebourg
Ste. Mère Eglise
Carenton
Périers
Lessay
St. Lô
Isigny
Port-en-Bessin
Bayeux
Caumont
Vierville-sur-Mer
St. Laurent-sur-Mer
Colleville-sur-Mer
Arromanches-les-Bains
Courselles-sur-Mer
Lion-sur-Mer
Ouistreham
Caen
Troarn
Cabourg

Map 2

N

0   5   10   15   20 km.
0   5   10   15 mi.

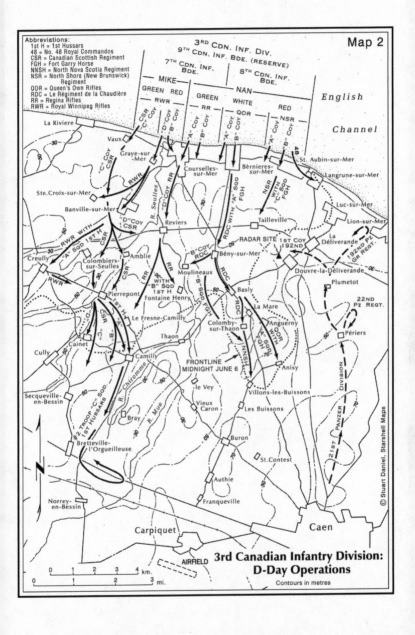

Map 2

Abbreviations:
1st H = 1st Hussars
48 = No. 48 Royal Commandos
CSR = Canadian Scottish Regiment
FGH = Fort Garry Horse
NNSH = North Nova Scotia Regiment
NSR = North Shore (New Brunswick) Regiment
QOR = Queen's Own Rifles
RDC = Le Régiment de la Chaudière
RR = Regina Rifles
RWR = Royal Winnipeg Rifles

3RD CDN. INF. DIV.
9TH CDN. INF. BDE. (RESERVE)
7TH CDN. INF. BDE.
8TH CDN. INF. BDE.

MIKE — NAN
GREEN | RED — GREEN | WHITE | RED
RWR — RR — QOR — NSR

English Channel

La Riviere
Vaux
"C" COY CSR
Grave-sur-Mer
Ste.Croix-sur-Mer
Banville-sur-Mer
RWR
Courselles-sur-Mer
Bèrnieres-sur-Mer
St. Aubin-sur-Mer
Langrune-sur-Mer
Luc-sur-Mer
Lion-sur-Mer
La Délivrande
192ND PZ GR. REGT.
Douvre-la-Délivrande
Plumetot
R. Seulles
Reviers
"D"COY CSR
Taillerville
RADAR SITE 1ST COY 192ND
Bény-sur-Mer
Creully
Colombiers-sur-Seulles
Amblie
Moulineaux
RDC
Basly
RDC
La Mare
22ND PZ REGT.
Périers
Pierrepont
RR WITH "B" SQD 1ST H
Fontaine Henry
1ST H
Le Fresne-Camilly
Colomby-sur-Thaon
Anguerny
OOR WITH "A" SQD FGH
Anisy
Cully
Cainet
Thaon
FRONTLINE MIDNIGHT JUNE 6
Villons-les-Buissons
21ST PANZER DIVISION
Secqueville-en-Bessin
Camilly
R. Chiromme
le Vey
Les Buissons
Bray
Vieux Caron
R. Mue
Buron
St.Contest
#2 TROOP "C" SQD 1ST HUSSARS
Bretteville-l'Orgueilleuse
Authie
Franqueville
Norrey-en-Bessin
Carpiquet
Caen
AIRFIELD

© Stuart Daniel, Starshell Maps

0 1 2 3 4 km.
0 1 2 3 mi.

Contours in metres

3rd Canadian Infantry Division: D-Day Operations

CHAPTER ONE

On June 6, 1944, the largest amphibious invasion in history took place on the coast of Normandy in France. The previous night, 5,000 ships carrying 131,000 Allied soldiers had sailed into position. Also during the night, 23,000 more troops had landed by parachute or glider. With the dawn, the soldiers at sea would begin to land on five beaches. The 3rd Canadian Infantry Division and 2nd Canadian Armored Brigade would land on Juno Beach. On either side of the Canadians, British troops would set down on Gold and Sword beaches.

To the west of Gold Beach, Americans would storm ashore at Omaha and Utah beaches.

Code-named Operation Overlord, the Allied invasion had been in the planning for four years. Really almost from the moment that Germany had seized all of continental Europe and driven the British off. War had broken out in September 1939 with the German invasion of Poland. It had only taken nine months from then for Germany and its allies—Italy and Hungary—to conquer the rest of mainland Europe.

But Britain had held out. For almost two long years it fought on alone. Alone, except for the support of its Commonwealth nations— chiefly Canada, Australia, New Zealand and India. Then, on December 7, 1941, the Japanese attacked Pearl Harbor in Hawaii and destroyed most of the battleships of the powerful American Pacific Fleet. This drew the United States into the war on the side of Britain, while Japan allied with Germany.

Within weeks of America entering the war, its military planners joined the British discussions on how to launch an invasion of continental Europe. In August 1942, a small raid was attempted at Dieppe. Most of the troops involved were Canadian. The raid on the small French resort town was a disaster. Hardly any soldiers got beyond the beaches. Total casualties were 3,367. This included 901 killed and 1,946 taken prisoner. These losses were all suffered in just nine hours.

Dieppe proved to the Allied planners that they were a long way from ready to invade France by crossing the English Channel. Yet they also knew that this was the best path of approach. But before an invasion could take place, they needed to build up a huge army in England. They also needed a vast armada of ships and much special equipment.

In the meantime the war went on. The Allies landed American and British troops in French North Africa on November 8, 1942.

This led to the eventual defeat of the German Afrika Korps on May 12, 1943. The struggle in North Africa had raged for thirty-two months.

The Allies kept the pressure on Germany by invading Sicily on July 10, 1943. Included in this invasion force was 1st Canadian Infantry Division and 1st Canadian Armored Brigade. Sicily fell on August 17 after hard fighting. Less than three weeks later, the Allies jumped from Sicily onto the Italian mainland. Canadian, British and American troops started marching north into boot-shaped Italy. They faced bitter resistance from German troops, who had hurriedly occupied the country when the Italian government surrendered to the Allies days after the Allies landed on the mainland.

For a short time the Allies had hoped it might be possible to defeat Germany by advancing through Italy into the heart of Europe. British prime minister Winston Churchill called this an attack on Europe's "soft underbelly." It was soon clear that the underbelly was anything but soft, and that it would take years of slogging to get from Italy to Germany.

This added urgency to the plan to launch an invasion across the English Channel. So from the autumn of 1943 to the spring of 1944, the Allies gathered their strength in southern England. By late May they were ready. The French province of Normandy had been selected for the invasion because its many sandy beaches were not as well defended as those farther east and closer to England. Allied fighter planes had gained complete mastery of the skies over the European coast. Allied bombers were destroying railway terminals and vital roads leading to Normandy. The entire region was soon isolated from the rest of Europe.

The date of June 6 was selected because of the way the moon affected the levels of incoming tides. At this point in the monthly lunar cycle the tide was considered perfect for putting soldiers, tanks, artillery and vehicles ashore. If the invasion did not proceed on that day, it would have to be delayed for months. Despite a storm, the weather was deemed acceptable. And so, in the predawn hours of June 6, 1944, about 14,500 Canadians were aboard ships off Juno Beach. With the dawn, they would storm ashore. This is the story of what happened on the day forever to be known as D-Day.

CHAPTER TWO

A coin toss decided it. Two of the four Queen's Own Rifles companies would be part of the assault on Juno Beach. The four company commanders tossed coins to decide who would have the honor. The Dalton brothers won. They would each have the honor of leading the charge. But likely one or both would die. Majors Charles and Elliott Dalton were both brothers and close friends. Charles, commander of 'B' Company, was six years older and considered it his job to protect Elliott. The fact was, Elliott should not have been in the coin toss at all.

But when 'A' Company's commander fell ill at the last moment, he replaced the man.

Charles decided to try to stop this. He found Lieutenant Colonel Jock Spragge on the bridge of New Zealand passenger liner SS *Monowai*. Spragge commanded the Queen's Own. Fond of his men, he had decided on the coin toss that would determine who led the first landing wave. Unable to make the decision on his own, he let chance decide.

"Don't send Elliott in on the first wave," Charles said. "You know what it will do to our mother if we both die."

Spragge knew. The Queen's Own was a tight-knit Toronto regiment. Every officer knew the families of his fellow officers. Charles, who was thirty-three, had joined the regiment's cadets in 1925. Elliott had soon followed. Spragge had known the two brothers ever since. He had been in the Dalton home many times. "There's nothing I can do," he replied. Coins had been tossed. To set aside the result would be unfair to whoever replaced Elliott. Charles understood. So he did not argue as hard as he would have liked to. Instead, he returned to the ship's deck.

* * *

Charles and Elliott started getting their men ready. The Queen's Own numbered about 800. Each rifle company was 120 strong. Reveille at 0300 hours had given the troops time for breakfast. The ship's cooks had gone all out. They knew this would be many a soldier's last meal. Plates were heaped with sunny-side-up eggs, crisp bacon and toast. After breakfast, each man was offered a stiff tot of navy rum. Most accepted. Then they started assembling their gear.

At about 0530 hours, Charles guided 'B' Company over to the boxy assault landing craft (LCA) dangling from hoists on the ship's deck. Each LCA carried about thirty-five soldiers. It took ten LCAs to carry 'B' Company.

When the order came, they would be lowered to the sea and cast free. Charles remained on the ship. He wanted to talk with Elliott. There would be time to board before the craft were away. Then he would move right to its front. Charles was determined to lead the charge onto the sand.

Elliott's 'A' Company remained on the ship's deck. They had to wait for 'B' Company's craft to be lowered and cast off. Rope nets were draped down the ship's side. These led to where 'A' Company's LCAs were towed alongside. Each man was loaded down with about a hundred pounds of equipment. This included his weapon, lots of ammunition, grenades, emergency rations and water canteens. When the time came, they would awkwardly climb down the nets and jump into the LCAs. Once everyone was aboard, the naval crews would circle the LCAs about, form a line and make for the beach.

Charles and Elliott stood together. They looked toward the Normandy coast. There was nothing much to see. Well inland, a predawn glow indicated that the sun would soon rise. But it would be hidden behind thick clouds. Stormy weather had made for an uncomfortable night as the invasion ships had closed on the French coast. The seas remained rough. Larger ships rolled heavily in the waves. Smaller craft tossed about like corks.

Ashore, flames rose from where shells or bombs had started fires. More than 5,000 ships stood off the coast. Many were destroyers, cruisers, monitors, gunboats that fired explosive rockets, and battleships with huge guns. All had started firing toward the coast at 0500 hours. Bombers had also swooped overhead and dropped tons of explosives. The intention was to destroy the German fortifications guarding the five beaches.

At dawn, thousands of Allied soldiers would begin storming ashore. Americans would land on two beaches—Omaha and Utah. The British aimed at beaches code-named Sword and Gold.

These were on either side of the Canadian beach. Juno was a long stretch of sand running from Courseulles-sur-Mer, east past Bernières-sur-Mer, and on to St. Aubin-sur-Mer—three summer resort towns being torn apart by shells and bombs.

Charles tried to say something meaningful. Elliott also searched for the right words. Suddenly Charles groped about in his mouth and pulled out a stubby denture. He chucked it overboard.

"What did you do that for?" Elliott asked.

"If I'm going to die, I don't want to have that damned thing hurting me," Charles snapped. He was so tense that his teeth were grating, and the denture had rubbed the gum raw. Charles hated the denture anyway. Maybe when it was over, the army could replace it with one that fit properly.

Suddenly a megaphone sounded, and a voice warned that the assault craft were to be lowered.

"I'll see you tonight," Charles told Elliott.

"Yes," Elliott replied. "See you."

The two men shook hands. Then they parted and headed for their place in history.

CHAPTER THREE

June 6, 1944, was D-Day for the Allied invasion of Normandy. D-Day was simply code for an invasion from sea. But after this day it would forever be identified with the most historic sea invasion in history. D-Day was an all-or-nothing gamble. The Allies staked the future of the war on winning the five beaches. If they failed, or were unable to hold them after getting ashore, World War II would drag on for years. It would take that long to build a new invasion force. And the Germans would use those years to strengthen their defenses along the European coast.

The Allies counted on winning a toehold on the French coast. A toehold from which they could break out across France, smash into Germany and win victory. If all went as planned, the war could be over by Christmas 1944. That was the hope. But everything depended on being able to defeat the Germans defending the beaches. It was a battle that had to be won in a day. Tens of thousands of troops had to land before nightfall. Enough men had to advance inland to establish a protective band around the beaches. If this did not happen, the Germans would counterattack and throw the invaders back into the sea.

That image haunted the invasion's planners. British prime minister Winston Churchill woke regularly from nightmares in which the sea ran red with blood. The bodies of thousands of Allied troops washed back and forth with the tide. Churchill kept his fears to himself. He insisted instead that the invasion would succeed. But he remained terribly worried.

* * *

Churchill was right to be worried. The Germans defending the beaches were badly outnumbered and outgunned. But the Allies could only land small numbers of men in the first assault waves. These troops would be terribly exposed. They would pile out of the LCAs and then have to wade ashore. But first they would have to find their way through a maze of obstacles that extended about 1,200 yards from shore. Farthest out were rows of concrete and wooden poles braced by logs or steel rails. This created an obstacle six feet high. Behind this, lines of pyramid-shaped barriers marched in rows back onto the beach. These obstacles were made by bolting three concrete, steel or wooden bars together. Scattered in their midst were hedgehogs—sections of angle iron bolted together to form an X shape. Explosive mines were attached to most of the obstacles in the water.

Tangled rows of barbed wire stretched across the entire length of each beach. Behind this wire were fortifications called pillboxes. Their concrete walls and roof were so thick that only a direct hit by a very powerful shell or bomb would destroy them. Entry was through a steel door on the side not facing the sea. Narrow slits in the front and sides provided the Germans with firing ports. Most pillboxes housed machine-gun crews. But some had been built around a small artillery piece capable of knocking out any tanks that might be landed. These guns could also fire at the LCAs.

Farther back, more Germans were in dugouts, trenches and fortified houses. At Juno Beach, many of the buildings sheltered Germans and were linked by trenches. Inside the three villages and inland, mortars and artillery guns could fire well out to sea.

The Germans hoped, of course, to smash the invasion on the beach. But they accepted this might not be possible. So, extending six miles inland were more defensive lines.

Each line consisted of hidden positions where they waited to ambush the invaders.

* * *

Planning the invasion had been a huge task—one worked on intensively for almost two years. For months the assault divisions had trained for this single day. For Canada, the job went to 3rd Infantry Division. Over the years, the division carried out many mock landings onto English beaches similar to Juno Beach. It was soon nicknamed the "web-footed division."

But infantry alone could not win the beaches. They needed tank support. This required inventing a swimming tank. Developing it fell to 79th British Armored Division. Major General Percy Hobart, an eccentric but brilliant tank specialist, commanded the division. The Duplex Drive tank was a standard Sherman tank weighing almost 70,000 pounds. Not a simple thing to keep afloat. The DD tank was made buoyant by circling it with a collapsible canvas screen mounted just above the tracks. Attached to the screen were thirty-two equally spaced four-inch-diameter tubes. When these tubes were filled with compressed air, they swelled like sausages. The screen was pulled upward to a height one foot above the tank turret. The air kept the heavy tank from sinking. Two propellers were installed at the rear of the tank. Powered by the Sherman's engine, they gave it a top speed of six knots.

The DD tank was only capable of staying afloat for short distances in a fairly calm sea. Rough water easily swamped it. If the screen collapsed on any side, the tank almost immediately sank. When the DD grounded, its crew dropped the screen. Once the screen collapsed, the tank's 75-millimeter main gun or either of its two machine guns could fire.

For the assault on Juno, two Canadian tank regiments were equipped with DD tanks. The Fort Garry Horse and 1st Hussars of

2nd Canadian Armored Brigade would land alongside the assaulting infantry regiments of 3rd Division. Two squadrons from each regiment manned DD tanks and would go in with the first assault wave. The third squadron kept its standard Shermans and would arrive at the beach aboard landing craft alongside the second wave. Seventy-eight DD tanks would land at Juno.

* * *

Just over a thousand infantrymen would be in the first assault wave. These came from five regiments. One Canadian Scottish Regiment company would land on Juno's extreme western flank. To its left, two companies of Royal Winnipeg Rifles would strike. One company would come ashore west of the inlet created by the Seulles River. This inlet provided safe harbor for the Courseulles-sur-Mer fishing fleet. To the east of the inlet, the second company would attack the village itself. Pushing into

Courseulles from farther to the east would be a Regina Rifles company. Another would win the stretch of sand between Courseulles and the next village along the way.

This was Bernières-sur-Mer. Capturing this village was the job for the two Queen's Own Rifles companies commanded by the Dalton brothers. East of here, the North Shore (New Brunswick) Regiment's two companies would assault St. Aubin-sur-Mer. The 1st Hussars would lend support to the Regina Rifles and Royal Winnipegs. Tank support for the Queen's Own and North Shores came from the Fort Garry Horse DD tanks.

Once the assault wave was ashore, a second Canadian wave of roughly equal numbers of infantry would land. These men would be from the same regiments involved in the first wave. They would be supported by the second wave of tankers from the 1st Hussars and Fort Garries.

The assault regiments were drawn from two of 3rd Division's infantry brigades.

From western Canada, the Can Scots, Reginas and Winnipegs served in 7th Brigade. The 8th Brigade was an eastern Canadian unit. It was formed by the Queen's Own of Toronto, the North Shores of northern New Brunswick, and Le Régiment de la Chaudière from Quebec. This last regiment would land behind the Queen's Own at Bernières.

Landing at the same time as the Chauds would be the division's artillery regiments. The artillerymen were equipped with American-made M7 self-propelled guns that fired 105-millimeter shells. Nicknamed "Priests," these guns had replaced the standard Canadian 25-pounder artillery piece. The motorized Priest ran on tracks and did not need a tractor to tow it to firing positions.

The Priests were loaded onto large flat-bottomed landing craft called LCTs. Each had been chained to the steel deck in such a way that the gun could fire toward shore on the way in. Ninety-six guns would blast away as the LCTs closed on the sand. Each would fire three shells every 200 yards. By the time the LCTs dropped their front ramps to let the Priests off, each gun would have fired 105 shells.

When the beach was won, the division's 9th Brigade would land and lead the advance inland. Its Stormont, Dundas and Glengarry Highlanders and Highland Light Infantry were both from Ontario. The North Nova Scotia Highlanders rounded out the brigade. Tank support would be provided by Quebec's Sherbrooke Fusiliers.

The Canadians were to advance about nine miles inland on D-Day. Their main objective was Carpiquet Airfield. This airfield had been turned into a major German fighter base. The Allies hoped to win the airfield easily and use it for their own fighter aircraft. That was the broad-stroke plan for Canada's role on June 6.

CHAPTER FOUR

Dug in behind the maze of beach obstacles were soldiers of the German Army's 716th Infantry Division's 736th Grenadier Regiment. Some were inside the concrete pillboxes. A larger number hunkered behind machine guns stationed in open pits. All the best routes to exit the beach were blocked by strongpoints. Most of these were defended by at least one 75-millimeter gun surrounded by protecting concrete. Thickets of buried land mines and great tangles of barbed wire encircled the strongpoints. The only entrance was usually a narrow gap at the rear. Wire covering this gap could be parted by someone who knew its location. But these gaps were not easily spotted.

Allied intelligence had detected at least nine such strongpoints on Juno Beach. Two guarded either side of the mouth of the Seulles River at Courseulles. One each defended Bernières and St. Aubin. The remainder overlooked the beach from the top of sand banks that ran between the three villages.

Aerial photographs revealed that the Germans were nearing completion of a network of dugouts two to three kilometers inland. Mortars and artillery pieces were spotted inside the dugouts. Intelligence officers had been unable to locate the heavier artillery batteries known to be within range of the beach. However, from other intelligence sources they knew there were several 75-millimeter batteries that each consisted of several guns. At least one 88-millimeter battery was believed to be in range. A battery of four extremely powerful 105-millimeter guns had also been reported.

* * *

The 716th Division were considered poor soldiers. Most were either younger than normal or older men considered unfit for better divisions. Some had been previously wounded and left with a minor disability. The division was trained to fight from defensive positions. This meant its men were not able to easily switch from defense to offence. Instead they would remain in their defensive positions until either killed or forced to surrender.

Poor soldiers they might be. But there were lots of them. The division consisted of two infantry regiments and one artillery regiment. It was believed to number more than 13,000 men. In reality, its total strength was 7,771. In the winter of 1944, many fitter troops had been sent to the Russian front. The 736th Regiment had three companies of men immediately facing Juno Beach. This was the largest number of Germans defending any of the five beaches. They numbered about five hundred.

The Canadian assault wave would outnumber them. However, the Germans fought from inside excellent fortifications. The Canadians would be completely exposed to their fire. Particularly the many machine guns, mortars and artillery pieces they manned. But Allied intelligence expected the beach defenses would be quickly wiped out. And that the advance inland would then proceed rapidly. How many troops from the 736th Regiment were inland was unknown. But they were not expected to seriously disrupt the advance from Juno.

CHAPTER FIVE

The Canadians off Juno Beach expected the German defenders to be obliterated before they even reached the beach. Throughout the night hundreds of RAF bombers had subjected the coast to a terrific bombardment. Then the naval ships had started firing. Shooting at Juno were two British battleships, a heavy cruiser and twelve light cruisers. There were also eleven destroyers and a good number of monitors, gunboats and rocket ships.

The destroyers raced close to the shoreline to fire at specific targets. Two were Canadian—

Algonquin and *Sioux*. At the same time as the destroyers closed in, 1,365 American heavy bombers dumped 2,796 tons of bombs on the coast. All five beaches were enveloped in smoke and flame. It seemed impossible anybody could still be alive on them.

Aboard *Algonquin*, ship's gunnery officer Lieutenant "Corky" Knight tried to zero the ship's four 4.7-inch guns onto a 75-millimeter gun battery hidden between seashore houses just west of St. Aubin. So much smoke and dust was thrown up by exploding bombs, he was unable to see whether *Algonquin*'s shells were hitting the target. "Goddamn Air Force is messing up our target," he growled.

His commander, Captain Desmond Piers, was cheerful. He kept spotting targets worth destroying. Two St. Aubin houses facing the beach looked ideal for German snipers. He had them smashed to pieces. Then a "summer hotel right on the beach" caught his eye. "We blew it to smithereens."

One thing puzzled Piers. *Algonquin* romped just off the beach. Yet not a single German gun fired. The sun was up. It was broad daylight. Out to sea the landing craft were clearly visible as they formed for the run in. *Algonquin* was totally exposed. Obviously the beach was about to be attacked. The Germans should be scrambling through dust, smoke and explosions to their positions. Any of the 75-millimeter, 88-millimeter or 105-millimeter guns could badly damage *Algonquin*. But no shells came. *Algonquin* continued blasting the beach while the landing craft streamed in.

Piers began thinking the naval and air bombardment had done its job. Perhaps the Germans were all either dead, wounded or too shocked to fight. He looked seaward to the landing craft struggling in rough seas. Maybe the only fight the troops would face was the one required to get ashore.

* * *

Probably the first man to die at Juno was Rifleman Andrew Galoway Mutch. The twenty-four-year-old from McCreary, Manitoba, served in the Royal Winnipeg Rifles. Historically, rifle regiments had been more lightly armed than regular infantry. A rifleman held the same rank as a private in regular infantry regiments.

Mutch was in the first assault wave. After scrambling down the rope net, he jumped across the gap between ship and LCA. He was picking himself up when a huge wave swept the LCA hard into the ship. One of its two engines stopped working. Wallowing in the waves, the LCA began struggling toward the beach. Badly underpowered, with water from each wave breaking over its bow, the LCA was in danger of being swamped.

It was a good two miles still from the beach. All the drenched and scared soldiers started getting seasick. Rifleman J.H. Hamilton suddenly saw Mutch climb onto the side of the LCA. He vomited into the sea rather than letting loose on the LCA's deck like the others. Hamilton watched a huge wave roll toward the LCA. He lunged to pull Mutch to safety. But the wave struck first. The LCA pitched hard to one side. Mutch went overboard. Weighed down by his equipment, Mutch sank without a trace. The LCA struggled on.

* * *

The stormy sea made it almost impossible to launch the Duplex Drive tanks. This sea was anything but the calm they were designed for. The plan called for the LCTs carrying the tanks to launch them 7,000 yards from shore, ahead of the LCAs carrying the infantry. The idea was that the tanks would reach the beach first and use their firepower to protect the infantry while they were exposed in the water and on the open beach.

Waves whipped by an eighteen-mile-per-hour wind rolled in at heights of three to four feet. Aboard the LCTs, the officers of the Fort Garry Horse and 1st Hussars tried to decide what to do. Finally it was agreed that the DD tanks would stay on the craft until they were only about 3,000 yards out.

The LCTs pressed on, bucking wildly in the waves. When they were within 3,000 yards, the naval commander in charge of the four LCTs carrying the Fort Gary DDs ordered them to keep going until they were just a couple of hundred yards from the beach. The DDs could swim from there.

No such luck for the 1st Hussars. Their naval commander ordered 'A' and 'B' Squadrons to launch at the 3,000-yard mark. Down Ramp Order bells rang. 'A' Squadron's Major Dudley Brooks shouted into his radio microphone for the nineteen tanks to roll off the LCTs. The Hussars fired up their engines. Then they hoisted the canvas screens. German artillery and mortar shells threw up huge plumes of water around the LCTs.

First off was Lieutenant Kit Pattison's tank. It bobbed into the water and settled nicely. None of the tank was visible. It looked like nothing more than a large rectangular canvas dinghy with three-foot-high sides.

Behind Pattison, however, a German shell tore away the chains that held the LCT's ramp at surface level. This made it impossible to launch the rest of the tanks at sea. A mechanical failure also prevented a second LCT from launching any. These two LCTs headed for shore. Their captains planned to unload the DDs right onto the sand.

Aboard another LCT, Lieutenant William Little's No. 5 Troop of 'A' Squadron launched. Little led the way. Waves immediately washed over the canvas screen. Two of the Sherman's five engines were flooded and died. Bursts of machine-gun fire tore through the screen at the waterline. But the Sherman remained afloat.

Just ahead of the LCT, a rocket ship loosed a full salvo of rockets. The recoil pushed the ship hard backward. This created a small tidal wave that slammed into the tank and collapsed the canvas screen. Little's Sherman immediately sank. All five crew bobbed to the surface. Suddenly a spray of blood spurted from Trooper George Stephen Hawken's body. He sank out of sight.

To prevent the other Shermans of No. 5 Troop being sunk, the naval commander steamed closer to shore, leaving Little and his remaining three men in the water. They would not be rescued until two hours later.

Only ten of 'A' Squadron's nineteen tanks launched. But all of 'B' Squadron got away. Almost immediately the Sherman commanded by Lieutenant Bruce Deans suffered complete engine failure. Everyone bailed out as the tank went down. Major J.S. Duncan tried to form the tanks into a line to make a kind of six-knot cavalry charge to shore. But the heaving seas left each tank crew fighting just to stay afloat. Sergeant Léo Gariépy saw the strut holding his rear sections of canvas break loose. Its total collapse was prevented by wedging a fire extinguisher between it and the tank hull. Bullets from the beach showered the tank and shredded the canvas screen. Two great pillars of water shot up around Duncan's tank, swallowing it. Gariépy saw only four heads in the water where it had been. Trooper Roswell Ernest Toffelmire drowned. Looking over his shoulder, Gariépy saw the other tanks churning along. He led the charge to the beach.

CHAPTER SIX

Aboard *Monowai*, the LCAs loaded with the Queen's Own 'B' Company were lowered and released. Then 'A' Company descended the nets. Company Sergeant Major Charlie Martin anxiously watched his men make the slow, awkward descent. Each soldier had to pause, clinging to the net, and measure the moment he should jump to the LCA. The best chance was when the craft slammed up against the ship's hull. Mistiming the jump could mean the soldier dropped between the two vessels—to either drown or be crushed to death.

Because of the rough seas, 'A' Company took longer than usual boarding. Naval officers bellowed for them to hurry. But the men knew the risk they faced and moved cautiously. Finally everyone but Martin was aboard. Martin was to make sure everyone in the company was taken care of. Looking down, he saw the last LCA had already cast off. Monkeying down the nets, Martin leapt toward it. He slammed against the gunwale. He would have fallen into the sea had two men not pulled him to safety.

CSM Martin bulled through No. 9 Platoon to take a position directly behind the drop ramp. On his right, Sergeant Jack Simpson nodded. The two men were good friends. Before being promoted, Martin had commanded this platoon. He knew every man well. Almost all of them had enlisted alongside Martin in early 1940. Simpson was a good sergeant. Martin trusted him to lead the platoon well. He also knew that Simpson was worried. He had a brother in the LCA carrying No. 7 Platoon.

All the LCAs were milling about. Martin wished they would start toward the beach. Every minute at sea added to the number of men becoming violently seasick. Martin saw Rifleman Bill Bettridge puke up his breakfast. Bettridge was one of 'A' Company's two snipers. The twenty-three-year-old from Brampton was tough as nails. He looked terrible. Martin wondered if he would prove useless when they landed.

In another LCA facing St. Aubin, Lance Corporal Gerry Cleveland of the North Shores was in the middle row, just behind the door. His platoon section was lined up behind him. There was a bench in the middle of the LCA, and the men were supposed to sit astride it like kids on a toboggan. But they were all standing, necks craned toward the beach. They wanted to see dry land, wanted to get off this damned boat.

"We'd be on top of a wave and could look down and see an LCA in a trough. The next thing you'd be down in the trough looking up, and there was water on either side of you, way up there high above." Cleveland had been raised in Yarmouth. Fishing was the town's economic mainstay. But his family were dairy farmers. He knew nothing of the sea. The waves looked thirty to forty feet high to him. He was terrified.

* * *

Also peering toward the beach from an LCA was Royal Winnipeg Major Lochie Fulton. Somewhere under the boiling dust and smoke was the precise spot his 'D' Company was supposed to land. Fulton wanted to find that spot. He wanted the company headquarters section set down precisely where the arrow drawn on his map indicated it should be. This would enable him to quickly lead the company's platoons forward.

Fulton could not believe the noise. *All the noise in the world*, he thought. Suddenly something started whacking the steel hull. Fulton realized it was German rifle and machine-gun fire. "Then you'd see a big spout of water come up, and it dawned on me it was artillery fire and this wasn't going to be a surprise. The Germans were awake and waiting for us."

* * *

To the east, the Queen's Own and North Shores led the way to the beach. The Fort Garry Horse DD tanks trailed because of the decision to take them virtually to the sand aboard the LCTs. Charlie Martin realized he could no longer see the thousands of ships out to sea. Nor were there any aircraft overhead. On either flank there was no sign of the other regiments attacking Juno. All he saw were ten little LCAs in a 1,500-yard-wide line. Ahead, the houses of Bernières appeared through the smoke and dust.

Martin saw the German fortifications. He saw the barbed-wire barriers and the

X-shaped obstacles that marched out of the sea up onto the sand. Suddenly it was deathly quiet. All Martin heard was the chugging LCA engines. Not a man spoke. It was eerily unreal. Then the LCAs broke formation. Each moved through the obstacles toward its assigned landing point.

Suddenly a single machine gun fired. A bullet chipped a piece of metal off the LCA. It slashed Rifleman Cy Harden's cheek open. A sailor slapped a bandage on the wound. "If that's the worst you get, you'll be lucky," the man shouted.

* * *

The Germans at Bernières held fire to prevent betraying their positions too early. Those at St. Aubin did the opposite. They threw everything at the North Shores while the LCAs were still well out to sea. In Gerry Cleveland's LCA, the men were still gawking toward the beach. They were trying to point out their landing spot in front of the row of shell-battered houses. Machine-gun rounds started hammering the front ramp. Everyone sat down in an instant. Heads ducked so they were well below the steel hull.

Nearby, Lieutenant Charles Richardson's platoon of 'B' Company had been in high spirits. Not a single man sick. They loudly sang a bawdy popular song. "Now, this is number one and the fun has just begun," it went. "Roll me over, lay me down, and do it again." They were just about to begin the chorus when an armor-piercing artillery shell sliced through the front ramp. A chunk of shrapnel slammed Sergeant Perley White in the chest. He was knocked sideways but was only winded. A deathly silence fell over the LCA. Richardson looked at his thirty-nine companions. Expressions were suddenly serious.

Gerry Cleveland didn't like being fired at. He told the section Bren gunner to stick the muzzle of his weapon through an open slot next to the front ramp. The Bren light machine gun was the most powerful weapon in each section. Cleveland wanted Private Gilbert Duke to fire at a machine gun raking their LCA. The LCA was just 200 yards from shore. Cleveland spotted colored tracer rounds from the gun flicking overhead. "Fire! Fire!" Cleveland yelled at Duke. The man just stood there with the butt of the Bren in his shoulder. It was as if he was paralyzed.

All along Juno Beach, German fire thickened. Everyone in the LCAs began to realize that the massive naval, artillery and aerial bombardment had failed to even dent the beach defenses. Queen's Own Rifleman Doug Hester turned to his comrade Doug Reed.

"There's the church," he said. "I thought it wasn't supposed to be there." The steeple was to have been blown off, the church smashed to pieces by shells. It stood defiant. Nothing more than a few shell scars were visible on its exterior. Then the two riflemen saw the five pillboxes on the seawall ahead. Each spat tracer fire their way.

* * *

To the west, the DD tanks of the 1st Hussars still struggled toward the shore. Eighteen-year-old Trooper Bill Bury was the co-driver in Sergeant James Malcolm "Ace" Bailey's tank. Everyone in the tank was seasick. Waves battered the canvas screen. Fearing they would collapse, Bailey ordered Bury, the gunner Al Williams, and his loader/wireless operator Larry Allen out of the tank to support the struts holding the screen up. They stuck to the job until machine-gun fire ripped at the screen a few hundred yards from shore. Without consulting Bailey, the men jumped back inside the tank. Bailey agreed with the decision. He had buttoned up his hatch and was using a periscope to look toward the beach.

Suddenly the tracks churned sand. The Sherman was ashore. They had made it. Bailey ordered the tank halted and the screens dropped. Looking to either side, Bailey saw his tank was directly between two pillboxes. Instead of having firing ports facing the sea, however, these had ones that enabled them to fire along the length of the beach. Each pillbox protected a small artillery gun. Had either been able to fire forward, they could have knocked out Bailey's Sherman. Instead, they were helpless.

Williams fired at the pillboxes and any other German target Bailey spotted. Each time Allen fed another 75-millimeter shell into the gun's breech, cordite stench and smoke filled the turret and made him puke.

The tankers failed to notice the rapidly rising tide until water gushed into the engine compartment and drowned several motors. Then Bury shouted that water was threatening to drown him and the driver in their compartments. Bailey ordered the tank farther up the beach. But the remaining engines were too gutless to pull the Sherman out of the mushy sand. Although stranded, they decided to stay with the tank. They would fight as long as possible.

CHAPTER SEVEN

"**O**ur engines are wide open, and we'll take you in as far as we can," the commander of the LCAs carrying the Royal Winnipegs shouted in Major Fulton's ear, as a constant spray of bullets rattled the hull. Fulton was reminded of hailstones hammering the tin roof of a prairie shack back home.

He and the others in the front stepped closer to the ramp. Those men in the row behind edged back to give more space. Or perhaps it was an instinctive shrinking away from what was about to happen. With a shriek of chains the ramp fell. Fulton took one great charging stride.

He expected water no deeper than his boot tops. Instead, he plunged into icy water up to his waist. Fulton nearly sprawled face-first. Behind him the LCA was high and dry. It was hung up on a shoal that the naval commander had mistaken for the beach.

'D' Company's headquarters section was hot on his tail. Fulton was trying to sprint. But the weight of equipment and drag of water slowed him to an old man's shuffle. Bullets struck the water. Each round left a little ring like that of a skipped stone. He had the curious thought that it might be possible to step over the skipping rounds and not be hit. Men on either side of him stopped for no reason. They slumped into the water as if tripped or wanting to sit and rest a moment. As one fellow fell, Fulton realized, *My gosh. He's been hit.* Suddenly the water was only knee deep. Fulton splashed free of the sea and ran faster than ever before through streams of tracer fire ripping the length of the beach.

Nearby, the LCA from which Rifleman Mutch had fallen overboard and drowned landed. Rifleman Philip Genaille stood in front of Rifleman J.H. Hamilton. Genaille was the front man in his section's row. Hamilton looked over Genaille's shoulder as the ramp fell. He saw a single tracer round flickering toward them. He realized it marked the approach of a machine-gun burst only when Genaille grunted and his stomach was torn open. The man fell dead. Hamilton stepped over his body and charged for the sand dunes ahead. The hot blast of an explosion struck him from the side. It was followed by the piercing agony of a chunk of shrapnel lodging in his right nostril. Hamilton staggered to the cover of the dune, collapsed and passed out.

* * *

To the right of the Winnipegs, the Canadian Scottish Regiment's 'C' Company set down on the extreme west flank of Juno Beach.

The company was loaded on seven LCAs. The craft managed to weave between the X-shaped obstacles and drop the Can Scots just six feet from the beach. As the ramp went down, Lieutenant Roger Schjelderup could see the open gray beach with not a person in sight. "We were the first to land, and over the beach somewhere was the enemy. There was machine-gun fire coming from the left front as we disembarked at the double. So skillful had been the landing that we were able to leap ashore without getting our feet wet."

Schjelderup's No. 13 Platoon's job was to cross the beach and cut a path through barbed wire. Once through the wire, it was to take out a concrete pillbox. Inside the pillbox was a 75-millimeter gun and several machine guns. This pillbox guarded the extreme western flank of Juno Beach. Left alone, it could slaughter the Can Scots.

Yet as Schjelderup led his men in a charge, no machine-gun tracers or muzzle blast came from the narrow slits of its firing ports. From off to the left, machine guns were firing. Some of his men were being struck down by them. But the facing pillbox remained silent. The men at the front of No. 13 Platoon went to work with wire cutters, snipping a path through the barbed wire. They grunted with the effort, casting furtive glances toward the pillbox. Everyone expected to be torn by bullets.

Then the gap was open. The leading section dashed through to the firing slits. Men wrenched grenades free. Others jabbed barrels of Sten submachine guns or Bren guns into the openings. Nobody fired a gun or threw a grenade. Their sergeant had risked a glance inside and saw nothing but some German corpses and abandoned equipment. This was one of the few pillboxes the great bombardment had actually put out of action.

The Château Vaux stood a short distance inland. It was the Can Scots' main objective. The large building was located in a wooded park. Hidden in the park grounds were German snipers and machine-gunners. No. 15 Platoon's task was to clear the park and take the château. To gain its objectives the platoon had to cut paths through a maze of barbed-wire entanglements. Snipers in the park fired the whole time. Two bullets struck Lieutenant Francis Gordon Radcliff. He fell, mortally wounded.

Several machine guns began firing from high ground to the château's right. Lieutenant D.A. "Sandy" Hay saw that No. 15 Platoon was in serious trouble. He ordered his No. 14 Platoon to take out the machine-gun positions. Corporal William George Ritchie led his section in a wild charge that collapsed when he was killed.

Private B.M. Francis saved things. A British Columbia First Nations man, Francis was a crack shot. When he fired his rifle, a German sniper died. He even killed one man with a snap shot from the hip at a range of fifty yards.

By the time Francis fell, wounded by a German sniper round, resistance right of the château had ceased.

Schjelderup's men reinforced No. 15 Platoon. The Can Scots threw out withering fire to force the Germans in one position to take cover. Meanwhile, a single section of men would close in on the position. Just before they moved into the line of fire, the rest of the Can Scots stopped shooting. Before the Germans could recover, the section of men was upon them. It was an effective but costly tactic. 'C' Company suffered heavy casualties reaching the château. When they finally had it surrounded, Major Desmond Crofton readied his men for another grim round. Two men carried flamethrowers. "Burn the place down if there is too much opposition in the building," he told them. But first a couple of grenades were thrown through windows. Seconds later the Germans inside surrendered.

The Can Scots faced more stiff fighting clearing the woods. Crofton consolidated the survivors of 'C' Company about 1,400 yards off the beach. It was not yet 0830 hours. According to plan, the rest of the regiment would soon land on the beach behind. To see if they were coming ashore, Crofton walked to the eastern edge of the woods. From there he could see all of Juno Beach. There was no sign of other Can Scots. That didn't alarm him. It was early.

What alarmed Crofton was the sight of the Winnipeg Rifles in front of the little hamlet of Graye-sur-Mer. The Winnipeg regiment was nicknamed the Little Black Devils. This was because their regimental crest included a wicked-looking little devil waving a spear. Crofton realized the Devils were being cut to pieces. He could also see a large force of German infantry milling around the inland villages of Ste. Croix-sur-Mer and Banville-sur-Mer. If they counterattacked the Devils at Graye-sur-Mer and Courseulles-sur-Mer, the entire sector of Juno Beach being assaulted by the 7th Infantry Brigade would be in danger of being overrun by the enemy.

Crofton sent a runner to find the naval Forward Observation Officer who had landed with his company. He wanted the naval FOO to get the battleships and cruisers offshore to give the Germans inland a pasting. When the guns ceased firing, he would launch 'C' Company against the enemy and drive them off. Doing so should give the Devils time to win their fight for the sand.

* * *

From where he was, Crofton actually only saw the area where the Little Black Devils' 'B' Company was landing and the section of Juno assigned to the Regina Rifles. He was unaware that Major Fulton and 'D' Company had managed to dash across the sand to the cover of dunes in front of Graye-sur-Mer.

Their casualties were surprisingly light. Now the company sheltered amid the dunes to escape murderous cross fire ripping the length of the beach. This fire came from a pillbox positioned at the mouth of the Seulles River.

The pillbox didn't worry Fulton. Its fire was a nuisance. Already his men were far enough up the beach that the machine guns in it were unable to fire effectively at them. Fulton planned to keep pushing inland. The pillbox could be sorted out later. But he was badly worried about the condition of 'B' Company on the left. It seemed those men were pinned down and being shredded.

To his relief, the DD tank commanded by Major Dudley Brooks of 'A' Squadron, 1st Hussars, ground ashore at that moment. Right behind were three other Shermans. Fulton ran to the tanks. He shouted up at Brooks, "Dud, I think there's nothing but minefields and wire in front of us. We've got to blow that up to get through. But I think 'B' Company needs a lot more help than we're going to need, so go help them."

Fulton turned at the sound of explosions behind him. He saw that some of his men had already blasted a route through the wire with bangalore torpedoes. These were long steel pipes filled with explosives. A man stuck the pipe deep into the wire and then lit a fuse at one end. When the fuse burned down to the detonator, the explosives went off—tearing the wire apart.

'D' Company wasn't waiting on its commander. The men were all streaming through the gap in the wire. Without waiting for a reply from Brooks, Fulton dashed after them.

* * *

Seven 1st Hussars tanks had made it to the sand, and three were already fighting alongside 'B' Company. These tanks had come under immediate fire from German artillery.

Captain J.W. "Jake" Powell's Sherman had weaved through a maze of beach obstacles draped with powerful anti-tank mines to gain the beach. Just as he dropped the canvas screen, a 50-millimeter round sliced halfway through the Sherman's main gun. Despite the loss of the main gun, Powell ordered the tank to charge the German gun. It was a straight line to the enemy gun position. Powell had his gunner firing the machine gun mounted next to the main gun. Another shell rang off the tank's hull, and shrapnel wounded Powell in the hand. But he continued to lead the charge until the Sherman closed right up on the fortification and killed the gun crew. His courage earned a Military Cross.

'A' Squadron's Lieutenant Red Goff, meanwhile, had led his three Shermans against a concrete fort dug into a sand dune. Inside the fort was a 75-millimeter gun. To get to the enemy position, the tanks had to wade across an oxbow of the Seulles River. As the tank commanded by Corporal Henry Andrew Pockiluk bulled through the water, it was disabled by a German round. Pockiluk and his crew safely escaped the tank. But they were mowed down and killed by several machine guns dug in around the German gun.

The remaining two tanks quickly knocked out the German gun with a vengeance and mercilessly slaughtered the machine-gunners who were raking the beaches from the shelter of buildings. This fortification silenced, the rest of the 1st Hussars from 'A' Squadron turned their full attention to helping the battered 'B' Company.

* * *

Getting ashore had been almost impossible for the Devils of 'B' Company. Their LCAs had sailed into heavy machine-gun, shell and mortar fire while still 700 yards from the beach. As the ramps went down, the men saw they faced five thirty-foot-square reinforced concrete blockhouses with numerous machine-gun positions between them in concrete strongpoints among the sand dunes.

Rifleman Jake Miller's platoon was dropped fifty yards from the beach in chest-deep water. Men started getting hit by bullets all around him. They just sank beneath the waves. Lieutenant Rod Beattie went down in calf-deep water with a bullet in his spine. Miller threw himself in front of his platoon commander, lifted his Lee Enfield and fired several rounds at a firing slit in a nearby pillbox. A German inside fired back, and a bullet painfully grazed his left side. Then a mortar bomb exploded to his right and shrapnel sprayed him. One chunk, larger than the rest, lodged in his right knee.

Miller was waiting for another shot to kill him. That's when Rifleman Emil Saruk raced across the open beach and slipped behind the pillbox. Seconds later the gunfire from it abruptly ceased. The twenty-seven-year-old soldier had managed to get in through a back door and kill the Germans within.

As Miller started crawling painfully out of the water, Beattie cried, "Jake, don't leave me." Miller crawled back and tried to drag the lieutenant out of the water. The tide was coming in and Miller couldn't free Beattie from the increasingly soft sand. Miller yelled to Platoon Sergeant Bill Walsh to help get Beattie to safety. Walsh walked over, picked Beattie up like a child and carried him to the shelter of the sand dunes.

A few minutes later, Miller and some other men worked their way around to the back of the pillbox. They found Saruk lying dead in front of the open back door. A cluster of dead Germans lay inside.

The beach was strewn with bodies. Others hung in the wire fronting the pillboxes. But there were also riflemen out past the wire and in among the fortifications now. Standing tall on the beach so his men would see him was 'B' Company's commander, Captain Phil Gower. He had lost his helmet. Bareheaded, he strode from one group of men to another. Gower directed each toward an enemy position. One after another, the enemy guns were silenced. But the cost was high. When the last fortification was eliminated, Gower had only twenty-six men. All platoon commanders were either dead or wounded. Gower won a Military Cross.

CHAPTER EIGHT

Immediately left of Gower's men, Regina Rifles 'A' Company had also gone straight into a meat grinder. They landed directly in front of a gun emplacement with four-foot-thick walls of reinforced concrete. Inside was an 88-millimeter gun. And on either side of this structure were heavy machine guns protected by concrete bunkers.

As Major Duncan Grosch ran out of the surf, his right leg buckled and he pitched in agony onto the sand with a machine-gun round in his knee. Everywhere men were falling dead or wounded. The tide was flowing in, and Grosch knew he had to move or drown. Ignoring the burning pain, he crawled free of the water. The pain was terrific. He pulled out the morphine vial that each officer carried and gave himself an injection. The morphine was just kicking in when he realized the tide was again rising over his body. Grosch struggled another two or three feet up the beach. The drug was making him woozy. He rolled onto his back, no longer caring about the rising water. Suddenly two men grabbed either arm and dragged him to the protection of a seawall that ran in front of Courseulles. Grosch realized the knee wound likely meant his war was over.

But his second-in-command's war had just begun. Captain Ronald Shawcross had joined the regiment in 1936 at age twenty. He enlisted as a private and had risen from the ranks to become an officer. When the ramp of his LCA had dropped, all six men in the two front rows had been shot down. Shawcross had dragged each man back into the craft to save them from drowning. Then he dashed after his platoon. Mortar rounds were exploding. On either side, men were being bowled over by explosions. Others were falling, bodies riddled by shrapnel. Shawcross gained the seawall and crouched behind it. Only four of his men had got across the beach.

'A' Company's survivors were strung out behind the seawall. They were pinned down by heavy fire from fortifications in front of houses that bordered a wide promenade. The seawall butted up against it. Two large rows of barbed wire ran along the promenade. Machine guns to the right and left of the Reginas could fire down the length of the gaps between the rows. One man jumped onto the promenade and started picking his way through the wire. He was instantly shredded by bullets. Shawcross and his men were stuck.

* * *

'A' Company had suffered heavily just to get ashore. But 'B' Company encountered only light opposition. Major F.L. Peters and his men gained the seawall with only a few killed or wounded. Then they stood staring up at a sheer wall too high to scramble over. They had no ladders. No grappling hooks and ropes.

Suddenly a Sherman from the Hussars growled up and blasted a section of the wall apart. The Reginas grabbed hand- and footholds in the shattered masonry and dirt. They climbed onto the promenade and rushed into the eastern side of Courseulles. Peters got the men busy clearing houses. Through the smoke and dust boiling on the beach, he was unaware that 'A' Company was stalled at the seawall. He figured they were right alongside, pushing through the western side of the town.

But 'A' Company remained pinned down. Just one man had managed to slip through a gap in the wire. He reached the cover of one building facing the sea. Lieutenant Bill Grayson then considered his situation. From the back of the house a narrow alley ran directly to one of the fortified guns. But the alley was blocked by barbed wire. He saw an MG42 machine-gun position behind the wire. Getting past the gun seemed impossible. Every few seconds its gunner fired a long burst up the alley, even though there was no obvious target. Grayson suddenly realized the gunner was firing according to a time schedule rather than *at* something.

He timed the sequence and figured out how many seconds passed between each burst. When the gunner ceased firing, Grayson ran. The wire caught him, snagged his clothing and held him tight. No way could he get free before the gunner fired again. Helplessly, he looked at his watch. The second hand ticked relentlessly toward the moment when the gun would start again. Grayson braced for the impact of the bullets. But the second hand passed the moment.

Nothing happened. Grayson realized the gun crew was changing ammunition belts or clearing a jammed round. He tore clear of the wire, ignoring the wicked barbs that slashed flesh and clothes.

Sprinting to the pillbox, Grayson flung himself against its concrete side for cover. Unhooking a grenade from his webbing, he chucked it through an open aperture. When it exploded, Grayson kicked in the back door. He stepped in with pistol raised and saw Germans scrambling out another door. The last man out tossed a stick grenade behind him. The grenade skittered to a halt between Grayson's legs. Stooping down, he picked it up and hurled it after the Germans. After it exploded harmlessly outside, Grayson took off in pursuit. He zigzagged through a trench system that brought him to the main pillbox with the 88-millimeter gun inside.

Grayson peeked cautiously through the open doorway. His pistol was up. A whole

Mark Zuehlke

bunch of Germans inside started shouting, "Kamerad, Kamerad." They threw their hands up. Weapons dropped to the floor all over the place. Grayson jerked the pistol. He signaled them to come out. Thirty-five Germans tumbled out and surrendered to a single Canadian armed with only a pistol.

When the 88-millimeter fell silent, Shawcross seized the opportunity. He didn't let 'A' Company waste time cutting paths through the wire. "Jump over it," he shouted. By ones and twos the men rushed the wire, dived over it and rolled back to their feet. Shawcross led them into the trench system and the heart of the fortification. 'A' Company rooted Germans out of their holes, shot down men trying to flee, and finally the fortification was theirs. There were only twenty-eight of them from the 120 who had approached the beach little more than a half hour earlier.

Shawcross waved an arm. Twenty-eight men moved with weapons at the ready into the streets of Courseulles. Looking over his shoulder, he could see the LCAs of the second wave were approaching the beach. That meant 'C' and 'D' Companies would soon be ashore. Shawcross felt greatly relieved as he walked in among the buildings and lost sight of the beach.

* * *

Behind Shawcross, the second wave was in trouble. Two LCAs carrying men from 'D' Company slammed into mined obstacles. The explosions killed most of the crews and soldiers aboard. Those who survived drowned. Only forty-nine men of 'D' Company reached shore. The company had landed in the same spot that 'A' Company had touched down.

'C' Company fared better. Major Stu Tubb and his men came in where 'B' Company had landed. They did so without trouble. Tubb quickly led the men into the town. They met no real resistance clearing their assigned sector in the center.

Lieutenant H.L. Jones, meanwhile, had taken command of 'D' Company's remnants. Instead of heading into the town, Jones led his men around its western flank. 'D' Company's objective was a bridge two miles inland. Jones had no idea that 'A' Company was fighting hard for control of the buildings he went around.

Inside west Courseulles, Shawcross thought his men were doing pretty well despite their small number. They were closing on the last buildings. *Should be done soon*, he thought. Then 'A' Company started to be fired on from buildings behind them. Buildings that were almost back at the beach. Lieutenant Grayson grabbed three men and headed back. Germans had reoccupied the pillbox and were firing a heavy machine gun from it. Grayson and the three men opened fire. Ten Germans quickly poured out of the pillbox and surrendered.

Grayson turned and saw more Germans emerging from a tunnel. He realized they were using the tunnel to get behind the Canadians.

Destroyer HMCS Algonquin *fires a broadside toward targets on Juno Beach near sunrise, June 6, 1944.* (HERB NOTT, NA, PA-170770)

Troops jammed aboard an LCA start out across the English Channel for Juno Beach.
(DENNIS SULLIVAN, NAC, PA-129053)

Members of Le Régiment de la Chaudière descend scramble nets to board an LCA.
(RICHARD GRAHAM ARLESS, NAC, PA-169304)

Major Lochie Fulton, commander of 'D' Company, Royal Winnipeg Rifles
(DONALD I. GRANT, NAC, PA-131271)

Highland Light Infantry troops eat hurriedly just before landing on D-Day morning. (GILBERT ALEXANDER MILNE, NAC, PA-136980)

Infantry in LCA heading to Juno Beach. (DENNIS SULLIVAN, NAC, PA-132790)

At 1140 hours the Stormont, Dundas and Glengarry Highlanders wade onto Juno Beach. (GILBERT ALEXANDER MILNE, NAC, PA-136980)

By late morning, Juno Beach throngs with men and equipment, including engineers laying steel mats to help vehicles cross the sand. (FRANK L. DUBERVILL, NAC, PA-132897)

Just before noon, Major General Rod Keller (center) arrives on Juno Beach.
(FRANK L. DUBERVILL, NAC, PA-115534)

German troops under guard in front of the seawall at Bernières-sur-Mer.
(FRANK L. DUBERVILL, NAC, PA-133754)

Wounded soldiers lie in the shelter of a seawall on Juno Beach. (FRANK L. DUBERVILL, NAC, PA-133971)

Canadian troops gather below a knocked-out German machine-gun position built into the seawall. (FRANK L. DUBERVILL, NAC, PA-116532)

Le Régiment de la Chaudière begins the advance inland from Juno Beach.
(FRANK L. DUBERVILL, NAC, PA-131436)

Canadian troops muster on the St. Aubin-sur-Mer sector of Juno Beach.
(FRANK L. DUBERVILL, NAC, PA-128789)

German prisoners carrying wounded Canadian. (FRANK L. DUBERVILL, NAC, PA-132469)

An ambulance jeep rushes wounded back to Juno Beach. (KEN BELL, NAC, PA-129031)

After a short firefight, twenty-eight more Germans surrendered. That finished the fight for Courseulles. Grayson's courage earned a Military Cross.

CHAPTER NINE

"Follow me," Major Charles Dalton had gallantly shouted at 0812 when the LCA ramp dropped. The Queen's Own Rifles were landing square in the middle of Juno Beach, in front of Bernières-sur-Mer. Charles saw a large two-story house to one side. Then he saw only water. The major plunged to the sea bottom in eight feet of water. Under the weight of his equipment, swimming to the surface was impossible. So Charles held his breath and started walking. Several minutes later, his head broke the surface. Charles kept wading shoreward. Soon the sea was only waist deep. He noticed with dread that the water to his right was whipped by bullets. The soldier closest to him on that side staggered as four slugs punched ragged holes in his chest and stomach. He flopped lifelessly into the sea. Looking past the stricken man, Charles realized every man in that direction floated lifelessly. Yet he remained untouched.

The soldiers to the right of Major Dalton had been caught in a maelstrom of fire from a concrete fortification directly ahead. He survived only because he was just inches outside the maximum arc of the machine guns inside.

Sergeant Fred Harris had led No. 10 Platoon off an LCA into the kill zone. He landed in waist-deep water and was immediately killed by a burst of fire. The three men in front of Rifleman Doug Hester died as they went out behind Harris. One was his friend, Rifleman Doug Reed. Hester plunged into water frothing with blood. He wallowed after Corporal John Gibson. The corporal seemed bulletproof.

Hester and Gibson reached the seawall. A machine-gun burst shredded the corporal's pack. Gibson grinned. "That was close, Dougie."

"Yes, Gibby, there goes your lunch," Hester joked. "We'll have to share."

Suddenly Gibson pitched over as a second burst killed him. Panicked, Hester scrabbled up against the cover of one wall of a pillbox. The machine gun inside was raking the beach. Hester saw Rifleman Ted Westerby staggering across the beach under the weight of a ladder. They were to have used it to scale the seawall. Three slugs punched into the man. Westerby fell dead in a spray of blood.

Hester decided to climb onto the pillbox and drop a grenade down an opening on the roof. But suddenly a hand darted out of the same opening and flipped a grenade out. It landed about four feet from his left foot. Hester doubled up, trying to make himself as small as possible. When the smoke cleared,

Hester was amazed to discover that only a tiny chunk of shrapnel had nicked his Achilles tendon. Abandoning the solo attack on the pillbox, Hester looked around for help.

The only men he saw still alive were gathered around Charles Dalton about a hundred yards away. Hester ran to join them. Dalton was standing with a rifle shouldered. He carefully aimed single shots toward the pillbox Hester had just fled. As Hester reached the group, a slug struck Dalton in the head. The major went down, blood spurting. Stretcher-bearer Alex Greer was immediately at his side. He discovered the bullet had glanced off Dalton's skull. Quickly he bandaged the deep furrow.

'B' Company had been decimated in a matter of minutes by the fire from the pillbox. Sixty-five men were either dead or wounded. Dalton knew more would die unless the pillbox was silenced. Drawing his revolver, he sprinted for it. His head throbbed. Blood leaked through the bandage, ran down his face. Dalton didn't run directly at the pillbox. He came at it from an angle to keep out of the machine gun's arc of fire. Charles slammed his back against the concrete. He gasped for breath, wiped the streaming blood from his face, then worked his way carefully around the back of the pillbox. When he tried the door, he was surprised to find it wasn't bolted from inside. Dalton stepped in and shot the Germans manning the machine gun before they could turn. Dalton's singlehanded attack won a Distinguished Service Order.

* * *

On 'B' Company's right flank, Major Elliott Dalton's 'A' Company had also gone straight into a shredder. As the LCA carrying Elliott gained the beach, the man steering it had been shot dead by a bullet between the eyes. The LCA careened on until it slammed up onto the sand. The ramp fell and Elliott yelled for his men to get out.

Company Sergeant Major Charlie Martin made sure 'A' Company did.

"Move! Fast! Don't stop for anything! Go! Go! Go!" he bellowed over his shoulder. Ahead was the tall half-timbered house that Charles Dalton had seen earlier. It was flanked on either side by a pillbox. Streams of machine-gun fire spewed out at the men on the sand. Sergeant Jack Simpson was cut down. Then someone stepped on a mine and riflemen Jamie McKechnie, Ernie Cunningham and Sammy Hall died. The blast wounded Rifleman Jack Culbertson.

Martin ran for a gap in the seawall left to allow the Germans to bring vehicles onto the sand. 'A' Company's two snipers were on either side of him. A single machine gun covered the gap. The man behind the gun was waving an arm wildly. Martin figured he was trying to get someone to bring him more ammunition. The three men charged the gun. They were firing from the hip. Fearing the German would get the gun going before they reached him, Rifleman Bill Bettridge abandoned the charge. He raised his rifle, took careful aim and killed the gunner with a single shot.

The three men ran through the gap and into the backyard of the half-timbered house. Behind it was a railroad station. This was an important Queen's Own objective. The way through was blocked by barbed wire strung along the tracks paralleling the beach. Martin, Bettridge and Rifleman Bert Shepherd dived into the cover of a ditch.

From here, Bettridge saw Rifleman Herman Stock, a twenty-two-year-old from the Wahta Mohawk Reserve, standing astride the rail tracks. Stock was a tall, powerful, Bren gunner. He had cut his hair Mohawk fashion for the invasion. Everyone else was crouched, lying flat or running to avoid presenting a still target. But Stock stood there, glaring toward the houses of the town. He seemed to be looking for a German to kill. The moment ended when a hidden sniper shot the man dead. Bettridge watched him fall. Then he hunkered deeper into the ditch. Bullets chimed off the barbed wire above him.

Martin was on Bettridge's right and Shepherd to his left. There was a space of about five feet between each man. Martin shouted to Bettridge, "Watch for these wire cutters. I'm going to throw them to you, and you throw them to Shep and tell him to cut a hole through that wire." Once that was done, Martin would feed what was left of the platoon through the hole. They could then take the rail station.

Shepherd bellowed, "You tell him to go fuck himself. He's making more money than we are."

Knowing Shepherd loved an argument, Martin started snipping. Soon he had a hole wide enough to crawl through. Fifteen men followed him through it. They crawled into a meadow of three-foot-high grass. The grass provided excellent cover. Unable to see the Canadians, all the Germans could do was fire randomly.

* * *

Martin and the men had almost reached a row of buildings next to the rail station when they ran out of cover. An open stretch of ground lay before them—ground surrounded by signs declaring it was a minefield. The only way forward was through the field. So Martin stood up and started walking. His men were right behind. At a steady walking pace it was sometimes possible to see where a mine had been put in a hole and covered over with earth. Martin and the men wanted to run. The Germans were throwing a lot of bullets their way. Each man was beginning to wonder whether it was better to be killed by lead or blown up by a mine.

Ten paces into the field, Martin heard a telltale click. He had depressed the detonating trigger of a Schützenmine. Lift his foot and the detonator would set off the mine. A canister loaded with 350 ball bearings would bounce three feet into the air ahead. The ball bearings would rip his guts open. As long as he stood still the mine was harmless. He gestured for the others to keep going. They slipped past and quickly gained the cover of the buildings.

Martin was calm. He could beat the mine. All he had to do was drop to the ground right beside it. The mine would bounce up above him and spray the ball bearings harmlessly in all directions. As Martin made his move, a bullet struck his helmet. The slug pierced the steel and spun round and round with such force inside the liner that it tore the helmet clear off his head. Luckily, the bullet also knocked Martin down. The mine exploded above him. Leaving the helmet behind, Martin fled. He joined his small group and led them warily into the streets of Bernières.

CHAPTER TEN

The North Shores landed east of the Queen's Own. Their objective was St. Aubin-sur-Mer. Lance Corporal Gerry Cleveland jumped into waist-deep water. Tracers zipped overhead. Swarms of machine guns and snipers fired from the two- and three-story houses facing the beach. Yet not a single man from Cleveland's 'A' Company was hit. "They were bad shots. Firing over our heads," he said later.

The houses lay on St. Aubin's western outskirts. A fifty-yard gap in the seawall separated these houses from the main part of town. The gap was plugged with a tangle of barbed wire. 'A' Company was to capture these buildings.

One of the first men ashore was Lieutenant M.M. Keith. He rushed for the seawall. Someone following stepped on a mine. A terrific explosion killed three men. Keith feared the base of the seawall was covered with mines. He broke left. The lieutenant made for the gap filled with wire. Private Gordon Ellis was close by with a bangalore torpedo over a shoulder. Keith yelled at him to blast a hole through the wire. Ellis shoved the pipe into the tangled snarl. Lighting the fuse, he dashed back to where Keith crouched out of the explosive's range. The torpedo's explosion set off a mine as well. Ellis was killed by the powerful blast and Keith badly wounded.

But a way was torn through the wire. Cleveland led his platoon section through the hole at a dead run. Machine-gun and rifle fire crackled at them. The men were forced to hug the walls for cover. But they were still exposed to the Germans firing down from the upper stories. The only way to fire back was to step away from the wall and into the open street. Nobody wanted to do that. So Cleveland's men were stuck.

Then a single Bren gunner dodged into the center of the street. He ripped the upstairs windows of a house with bursts of fire. While the Germans were ducking for cover, Cleveland and the others broke into the ground floor. They threw grenades up the stairs and lunged up them on the heels of the explosions. The Canadians went at the Germans with grenades, rifle fire and bayonets.

Cleveland's section repeated this technique to clear several more houses. Then they paused for a breather in an opening between buildings. Cleveland saw that the rest of 'A' Company had followed them through the gap. They were busy cleaning the Germans out of nearby buildings. Cleveland started to signal his men back into the smoke and confusion of gunfire and exploding grenades. He never finished the gesture because a mortar or artillery round exploded nearby. Shrapnel tore into the calf and ankle of Cleveland's left leg. Privates George McLeod and Alfred Blanchard fell dead. Everyone dove for cover. Mortar rounds fell all around. The moment the explosions quit, Cleveland's men took off to attack another house. Cleveland hobbled back to the beach and flopped down against the seawall. He figured his fight on Juno had lasted less than thirty minutes.

* * *

'B' Company, meanwhile, landed right in front of St. Aubin's center. All the buildings facing the beach were defended by snipers and machine guns. But a major concrete strongpoint posed a far worse threat. It enjoyed an exceptional command of the beach. The strongpoint sheltered a 50-millimeter gun, several machine guns and three 81-millimeter mortars.

Steel shutters and doors protected every opening. Trenches provided extra defensive space for German defenders. About a hundred were in the trenches or the strongpoint itself. They lived in a barracks buried underneath the strongpoint. Tunnels ran from the barracks out to surrounding houses. The Germans could easily move about without the North Shores seeing them.

Those in the strongpoint came to life the moment 'B' Company hit the beach. Lieutenant Charles Richardson's platoon set down right in front of the pillbox with the 50-millimeter gun. Machine-gun bullets kicked up sand all around his men as they dashed to the seawall. Their heaviest weapons were the Bren guns and a two-inch mortar. Rounds from either weapon type bounced harmlessly off the thick concrete walls. Richardson realized their only chance was to get around the strongpoint by taking the houses on one side. He led his men along the seawall and then made a dash for the nearest houses. It was a vain attempt. Heavy fire from the buildings quickly drove Richardson's platoon to ground.

Down the beach, Lieutenant Paul "Bones" McCann's platoon was also in trouble. The strongpoint jutted out beyond the seawall here. The platoon was left with nowhere to hide. Lashed by machine-gun fire, the men started bunching up. McCann stood up and yelled for the men to get over the seawall. They had to take one of the buildings next to the strongpoint. McCann got about two words out before a sniper round ripped into his arm. The slug passed through the arm, entered his chest under the armpit and then exited out the center of his back. McCann was spun around by the bullet's impact. Then a mortar round exploded. The concussion slammed the lieutenant flat on his face. He tried to lever himself up. But his left arm was useless, and he passed out.

Not far from where McCann fell, Captain Bill Harvey hunkered behind the wall.

He watched one Bren gunner after another fall to fire from the strongpoint. Then his two radio operators were killed. The radio was also wrecked. Harvey said later that he "could see the way in which the enemy had arranged his field of fire and had all the approaches covered with machine-gun fire. Snipers were cleverly located and could move underground from one point to another." All the North Shores could do was take cover and wait for their supporting tanks to land.

* * *

The boats carrying the Fort Garry Horse tanks were still closing on the beach. But the North Shores' second assault wave was ashore. Six-foot-one Major Ralph Daughney had jumped off an LCA into water that only came to his waist. Right behind was his radio man, Private Joe Ryan. Just five foot four, Ryan had nearly drowned, with water up to his chin. Soldier, radio, rifle and all other equipment were soaking wet. But he dogged Daughney's heels. Ryan had prayed silently to steady his nerves on the run in to the beach. But being on the sand was scarier yet. Men lay dead or wounded all over. And more fell every second.

Fortunately some engineers managed to brace a steel ramp against the seawall in front of 'C' Company. Daughney led his men up the ramp, and they dashed in among the facing buildings. Their objective was the church in the center of the town. 'C' Company started fighting toward its clearly visible spire. They broke into buildings and rooted out snipers and machine-gunners. No sooner was one building cleared than Germans sprouted up in houses beside it. A new round of fighting would begin. Finally, they reached the church. A nest of snipers in the spire had to be killed.

'C' Company had got past the German strongpoint on the beach and won its objective. The rest of the North Shores were still stuck in front of it.

* * *

But the Fort Garry Horse 'C' Squadron was now coming ashore. Four tanks had been lost at sea. Major William Bray formed the remaining sixteen in front of an opening in the seawall that provided the beach's only vehicle exit. The Germans had blocked it with mines. Engineers were working frantically with detectors to locate and clear them. But snipers made the work dangerous and slow. At about 0900 hours, Bray's patience snapped. He ordered the tanks to push through the minefield and into the town. Three Shermans were knocked out. The rest split up by troop and went to help the North Shores.

Also just ashore was Lieutenant Colonel Donald Buell. The North Shores' commander realized the strongpoint was too strong for Sherman tanks to crack. He sent for a Petard, and a few minutes later one clanked up. Its crew moved the converted Churchill tank virtually on top of the strongpoint. Then they opened up with its mighty twelve-inch gun, designed to destroy fortifications. The gun's special forty-pound square-shaped rounds smashed against the concrete walls. Great cracks opened up, and chunks of masonry flew in all directions.

While the Petard hammered the strong-point from the front, two Fort Garry tanks worked in behind it. The concrete was not as thick here, and they started chipping it to pieces. This combined fire threw the Germans into a panic. White flags sprouted out of various openings. Lieutenant Richardson and several men advanced to accept their surrender, only to have several North Shores cut down by sudden bursts of machine-gun fire.

A renewed attack led to another flurry of white flags. But the "North Shores had had enough of that trickery," Captain Harvey later wrote. "[They] went in with bombs, cold steel and shooting. They inflicted many times the casualties we had suffered and cleaned the place out." The vicious battle ended abruptly at 1115.

The surviving forty-eight Germans surrendered. At least that number had been killed inside.

St. Aubin was firmly in North Shore hands. Winning it had been costly. Lance Corporal Bud Daley and two brothers all landed with the regiment. Bud asked a passing sergeant about his brother Harold. "I'm afraid he got it," the sergeant said. Bud found Harold's body lying on the side of a road. He gathered up his personal belongings to send home. Then Bud heard his company officers shouting. They were ordering the men to form up for an advance inland. Bud forced himself to leave Harold lying there. He ran to join his company. Corporal Alden Daley also soon learned of his brother Harold's death. He was struck with "a terrible feeling of loss and a feeling of this is the real thing; there's no joke about this."

CHAPTER ELEVEN

All along Juno Beach the Canadians were starting inland by late morning. Despite heavy casualties, Juno Beach was theirs. They still faced fierce fighting. German artillery and mortar fire hammered the beach. It also dogged the advancing infantry and tanks. Beyond the beach, more German infantry hid inside defensive systems.

It had been expected that winning the beach would be difficult. Advancing inland was to have been quick and easy. The fight on the sand had taken longer than planned. By the time the coastal resort towns were clear, the Canadians were badly behind schedule. Their final June 6 objectives were about twelve miles away. The race was on. A race they thought could still be won.

A massive traffic jam had developed. Hundreds of men poured ashore. Vehicles stood nose to tail on the sand. Engines roared. Men shouted directions and waved their arms. There were infantry support vehicles. These consisted of the small, tracked Bren carriers and trucks. Some Bren carriers towed six-pound anti-tank guns. There were the self-propelled Priest 105-millimeter guns of the artillery regiments. There was an array of the specialized engineering vehicles. All the surviving tanks of the 1st Hussars and Fort Garry Horse were there, as were the 79th Armored Division's Funnies. There were ambulance jeeps emblazoned with red crosses and stacked racks of stretchers to carry the wounded from the battlefield. Trucks loaded with radios sprouted antennas. An army was pouring ashore and running out of shoulder room.

The seawalls and sand dunes limited routes off the beach. Wherever an exit existed, the Germans had sown hundreds of mines. Engineers worked to find and lift the mines while the men in the vehicles waited impatiently and the tankers fumed. Already the infantry was advancing. Each regiment was quickly entangled in firefights. They needed the tanks.

On Juno Beach's western flank the 1st Hussars of 'C' Squadron were to support the Canadian Scottish advance. The tankers watched helplessly as the rest of the Can Scots landed and joined the company that had been in the assault wave. Lieutenant Colonel Fred Cabeldu told his company commanders not to wait on the Hussars. They were to move. Major Desmond Crofton's 'C' Company was already almost a mile inland. It had closed on the village of Ste. Croix, breaking the

German counterattack that had threatened the Winnipegs. But Crofton radioed Cabeldu. The company had lost too many men to go farther alone, and it was unlikely they could fight off another counterattack. Cabeldu told Crofton to hold tough. The rest of the regiment was on the way. As Cabeldu strode along, he talked on the handset of the radio his signaler carried. Cabeldu called for the Hussars to marry up with him.

* * *

'C' Squadron's Captain Brandon "Brandy" Conron wanted to do so. The engineers in that sector of Juno were clearing mines from a single opening between sand dunes. A bend in the Seulles River added to the problem. It created a water obstacle that also had to be crossed. Conron went looking for another way off the beach. He found it about 200 yards to the left of the assigned exit. He led several Shermans through the gap. Then the tanks clawed up to the top of a last dune. The tankers wiped out some German infantry manning a small concrete fortification behind it.

Facing them was a thousand yards of heavily mined ground. On the other side, a rickety-looking bridge crossed the water. Conron jumped off his tank. As machine-gun slugs chipped the ground all about him, he dragged a tangle of barbed wire aside. The tankers were free then to enter the minefield. The Shermans lined up in single file. Conron jumped onto the lead tank. Its commander, Lieutenant Bill McCormick, pointed at the bridge. "You can't use that," he said. Conron shook his head in frustration. McCormick was right. A Sherman tank would collapse the thing.

A mortar round exploded beside the tank. Shrapnel peppered Conron in both legs. While the captain hugged the turret for protection, McCormick wheeled about and drove the wounded man back to the Regimental Aid Post.

Then McCormick led the squadron over to where the engineers still worked. Finally the exit was open. The engineers led the way through. They were followed by a specialized tank called an Ark. Instead of a gun turret, the Ark was topped by a steel ramp that could be unfolded, with the tank's hull providing the foundation. It trundled into the water and created an instant bridge. 'C' Squadron rumbled across. They caught up with Lieutenant Colonel Cabeldu a few minutes later. He walked in the midst of the Can Scots' 'A' Company. In quick order, the infantry-tank force reinforced Major Crofton and his 'C' Company.

Cabeldu swung the small force in between Ste. Croix and a village to the east. This was Banville. Clearing these villages would be left to the Royal Winnipeg Regiment. The Can Scots were to lead 7th Brigade's advance inland. They found the route hazardous, as they were moving through thick grain fields that appeared to be their only protection from many machine-gun posts.

In the middle of a field, a machine gun opened up on Private Jack Daubs and his section. The German gunner fired a long burst. Bullets struck down the lead man, but missed the one immediately behind. The third man was not so lucky. He fell dead, while the fourth lived, and the fifth also died. That man dropped directly in front of Daubs. Daubs looked over his shoulder to see the man behind him dying. Those still alive dived for cover and lay there until another platoon wiped out the machine gun.

Most of the German gun crews were not willing to die. They fired a few long bursts and then surrendered. Once disarmed, they proved incredibly passive. A single soldier could escort fifty or more back to the beach without any attempting to escape.

The Hussars of 'C' Squadron were amazed not to encounter any German tanks or self-propelled guns. They had a picnic steadily taking out machine-gun nests and entrenched positions whenever the infantry bogged down. The tanks scurried back and forth, working madly behind and on the flanks of the infantry.

* * *

Behind the Can Scots, the Winnipeg Rifles advanced through mortar and artillery fire of astonishing accuracy. Soon they closed on Ste. Croix and Banville. The Germans had abandoned Banville. But they held Ste. Croix in strength. Resistance was fierce until 'A' Squadron of the Hussars arrived. The Winnipeg war diarist was impressed by the tankers. He wrote, "[With] cool disregard for mines and anti-tank guns, [they] beat down the machine-gun positions and permitted 'A' Company to mop up and advance to the south [of Ste. Croix.]" The Little Black Devils pushed hard out of Ste. Croix. Hooking to the right of the Can Scots, they advanced toward Creully. Perched on a hill and built around an old castle, Creully was about four miles inland from Juno Beach.

On 7th Brigade's left flank, meanwhile, the Regina Rifles faced stiff resistance getting out of Courseulles. But French civilians rather than German soldiers were the problem. Hundreds of civilians poured out of cellars. They pressed flowers, wine and precious food on the marching men. Company commanders dashed along the line, pushing civilians back and warning the men not to drink the wine. By 1215 hours, the Reginas had reached the village of Reviers. This was about two miles inland. Here they stopped and waited for 8th Brigade to win its longer fights for Bernières and St. Aubin. Once the Canadian advance from these two towns began, they would join it.

CHAPTER TWELVE

The engineers at Bernières were delayed constructing exits through the seawall. This left ever more vehicles and men jammed on the beach with nowhere to go. Le Régiment de la Chaudière, 8th Brigade's French-Canadian regiment, was to lead the advance inland. It got off to a rough start. Almost every LCA had struck mines. All 'A' Company's crafts were sunk. Those men who didn't drown had to abandon much equipment in order to swim ashore. Every man in 'B' Company's No. 11 Platoon was either killed or wounded when a mine sank its LCA. Lieutenant D. Paré suffered serious wounds to his head and arms. Ignoring the pain, he got the survivors ashore. Those not too badly wounded were patched up and moved to where the regiment was gathering.

The Fort Garry Horse's 'A' Squadron was to support the Chauds. Captain Eddy Goodmand decided to escape the traffic jam by cutting across some open fields. "I came to one ploughed field and saw a sign reading *Achtung Minen*. Somewhere in the back of my mind I remembered an intelligence officer saying that often instead of mines the Germans put up signs to slow the enemy's advance. I decided that this was one of those times and went bowling across the field, only to blow up my tank, completely destroying the right track." He took over another tank and led the squadron through to the Chauds.

At about 0940 hours, 'A' Squadron, the Chauds, a battery of Priests from 14th Field Regiment, a heavy machine-gun section of Cameron Highlanders of Ottawa (MG), and the surviving Queen's Own Rifles clustered in an orchard immediately west of Bernières. Men and machines clogged the ground around the fruit trees.

The Chauds were pumped. When the civilians heard their liberators speaking French, they went crazy. Bottles of wine were passed. Flowers were thrown. Young women rushed to hug and kiss soldiers. The Quebecois dialect was very close to that of Normandy. Everyone understood the other perfectly. It was a reluctant bunch of Chauds who marched out of town and into the orchard. They would rather have stayed for a party than lead the rest of the Canadians into another battle.

All the activity in the orchard was not missed by the Germans. From Juno Beach the ground inland rose gradually. The Germans could see every Canadian move. They lashed out at the orchard with artillery and mortar shells. A hidden machine gun began firing.

Queen's Own Rifleman Jack Martin was in charge of one of the battalion's three-inch mortars. He had just set it up when a machine-gun burst ripped overhead. Martin and his teammates hit the dirt. Martin heard someone stomp up. He looked up to see Lieutenant Colonel Jock Spragge glaring down.

"For Christ's sake," Spragge barked, "you don't duck for every one of them." Martin sheepishly got behind the mortar. He began chumping out rounds toward suspected enemy positions. A section of Queen's Own riflemen, meanwhile, circled in on the machine-gun position and killed its crew.

Martin was twenty. A tough kid from Toronto's East End, he was just sixteen when the war started in 1939. He lied his way into the 48th Highlanders of Canada, only to find the regiment's bagpipers seemed to always be squeezing and blowing on the pipes. Finally he transferred to the Queen's Own to escape their squalling. Martin doubted the hated pipes would bother him now. He had spent years firing mortars. The hard thump of each round going out was steadily leaving him deaf. Martin punched out rounds faster than ever before—and realized he could hardly hear anything.

Four 14th Field Regiment Priests stood to his right. The closest was about a hundred feet away. Chauds formed by companies around the Priests, which were the first 14th Field Regiment guns ashore. Extra ammunition was strapped all over their hulls. Their long 105-millimeter shells were tied on in bundles. Cases of bullets for the infantry were strapped on in stacks. Even mines for the engineers hung by ropes off the hulls.

Suddenly the Priest closest to Martin's mortar exploded. It had been hit by an 88-millimeter shell. When the Priest exploded, so did all the shells, bullets and mines attached to it. Martin dived for cover, horrified to see a huge chunk of steel armor graze his mortar and then whirl overhead. The chunk landed about a hundred feet away and left a deep nick in the mortar tube. Later Martin often looked at the mark and was reminded of how close he had come to being "squashed like mashed potatoes." But he didn't think if it at that moment. Instead, he righted the mortar and got busy again, throwing rounds toward the Germans.

The 88-millimeter gun, meanwhile, fired three more shots. Two of the three remaining Priests died. The fourth Priest barely escaped. Its driver backed the gun into a lane that hid it. There were twenty-one men in the three Priests hit. Six died and another five were badly wounded.

'B' Company of the Chauds was also caught in the explosions. Lieutenant Raymond Lapierre and a dozen men died immediately. Several more were wounded. This reduced the company from about 120 initially to barely 40.

Major Hugues Lapointe of 'A' Company had spotted the German gun position. It was hidden beside a cemetery. Backed up by 'A' Squadron Shermans, his men overran the gun. Most of the crew were killed. The surviving three were taken prisoner.

* * *

Infantry and tanks then started up a long, straight country lane. They headed for Bény-sur-Mer. This village was about two miles inland. Just a thousand yards out, the leading platoon walked into a cross fire from several machine guns. On either side of the road were wide grain fields. Spreading out into those would get the men slaughtered. So they dived into the roadside ditches and hugged the earth.

Lieutenant Colonel Paul Mathieu sent scouts crawling into the fields. Their job was to find each gun position inside the grain. It was slow, dangerous work. The main Canadian advance was stalled. A long delay was inevitable. Yet Mathieu's radio messages to 8th Brigade headquarters downplayed this fact. Signals sent by 8th Brigade to Major General Rod Keller, who commanded 3rd Division, reported the advance proceeding. The pace might be slow, but it was still underway.

Keller faced a decision at that moment. It was 1050 hours. He was ready to send the reserve brigade ashore. This was the 9th Brigade. Originally the brigade's three battalions were to have landed in two packets. One would set down at Bernières, the other at St. Aubin. This would position the brigade well to leapfrog 8th Brigade. Another option was to land the brigade at Courseulles. But this would mean a longer advance route to their final objective of Carpiquet Airfield.

The general decided to go with the first option. He began issuing the orders. But the naval officer overseeing the landing said that St. Aubin's beach was too hotly contested.

The large strongpoint on that beach had yet to be eliminated.

Keller was anxious to get 9th Brigade ashore. It was obvious 8th Brigade was running out of steam. The 9th Brigade needed to take over the advance. So he ordered all of it landed at Bernières. As soon as the orders were given, Keller turned to Canadian reporter Ross Munro.

"It is hard fighting," he said, "but our troops are doing great. I'm committing the reserve brigade now and it is landing at Bernières, where the best beach exits have been made."

Munro was elated by the news. It seemed the Canadian assault on Juno was going far better than expected.

CHAPTER THIRTEEN

Not only the Chauds were stalled. The North Shores had finally marched out of St. Aubin at 1230 hours. They were hours behind schedule. Ahead, Tailleville was about a mile and a half inland. The troops advanced up a narrow road running through a wide expanse of grain fields. Small orchards and little cow pastures were scattered here and there. Fields were divided into large squares by thick hedgerows. These provided perfect shelter for German ambushes.

A twelve-foot-high stone wall surrounded Tailleville. It was three feet thick.

The Canadians could see only one building behind the wall—a tall, hulking château. Its upper stories provided a perfect observation post for the Germans.

Major Ralph Daughney's 'C' Company led the North Shores' advance. Daughney was optimistic. Earlier he had ridden a bicycle almost to Tailleville. Not a shot had come his way. Daughney hoped to march right through without anybody getting hit. He had a platoon out in the grain on either side of the road. The Fort Garry Horse's No. 5 Troop was using the road and was in between the two platoons. 'C' Company's remaining platoon and headquarters section trailed the tanks. The rest of the North Shore infantry and Fort Garry Shermans followed in a long line.

The Germans had not bothered shooting Daughney off the bicycle. Instead, they had lain low. Now they started sniping. Mortars and artillery also dogged the column. The advance would have stalled, but Lieutenant

William Little's tanks hammered the German positions with 75-millimeter shells and machine-gun fire. Often the tankers ground into the fields to destroy German positions at close range. Sometimes they just crushed the snipers or machine-gun crews under the tracks. Daughney told Little that "without his excellent and energetic support [my] company would not have been able to advance at all."

Daughney and radioman Private Joe Ryan ran, dodged and fell. They moved in rhythm with the incoming scream of mortar and artillery shells. Explosions ripped great gouges out of the earth. Ryan thought the shriek of shells was like a cry of agony, as if the earth was protesting being raped. "The smell of cordite and earth spewed up made me almost sick to my stomach."

Just short of the village, dense hedgerows surrounded a few small orchards. Machine guns hidden in the hedgerows raked 'C' Company. Men faltered. Many dived for cover.

The attack was collapsing. Something had to happen fast. Daughney sent a runner to his second-in-command, Captain Hector LeBlanc. Leblanc was to get Sergeant Albanie Drapeau's three-inch-mortar team to engage the German positions. Drapeau later wrote that LeBlanc "showed me the exact clump of trees he wanted fire brought down on. Luckily I made a quick correction in degrees and the first ranging rounds fell exactly where he wanted them. In a few minutes the mortars had quieted the German machine guns. Luck was with me that day for each time I was able to score direct hits."

One machine gun proved impossible for Drapeau's mortar. There was also no way anyone could get at it from where 'C' Company hid. Not without taking a suicidal risk. Private Herbert Butland took that risk. He charged, firing a Bren gun from the hip. The MG42 machine gun shrieked a long burst at the running Canadian. Bullets clipped the suspenders holding his web belt right off his shoulders. But miraculously not a slug scratched his flesh. Butland killed the gun crew with a lethal burst. His bravery was rewarded with a Military Medal.

* * *

The North Shores and Little's tank troop reached Tailleville. They stopped outside the high wall. Daughney was perplexed. It was as if he had been cast back to the medieval ages. He expected knights and archers to appear at any moment and lay siege to the massive wall and château behind. Daughney could find no way to get through or over the wall.

Men crouched against it. To fire at them, the Germans would have to crawl out on the wall's three-foot expanse. The tanks and North Shores farther back would kill any German who tried that. They could only toss grenades over. But they were throwing blind. Still, one grenade landed next to where Little stood outside his tank. Suffering multiple cuts, he was evacuated by stretcher bearers. By that time, Captain Alexander Christian had arrived with three more tanks. That brought the tank force up to six. Christian led them around the entire village. They fired shells over the wall, hoping to hit something.

The Germans struck back with rifle and machine-gun fire. Bullets ricocheted deafeningly off the steel hulls. Christian had his turret hatch open. This allowed him to peer out and better direct his tank's fire.

"Suddenly," he recalled later, "an impact like a sledge hammer hit the back of my head, and I slumped on the floor, but regained consciousness and felt better after a drink of water. A bullet had pierced my helmet, grazed the back of my head and had gone out the other side of the helmet." One of his men bandaged the wound. Then Christian went back to firing into Tailleville.

A few minutes later he spotted a 75-millimeter gun, several other, smaller, artillery pieces and an ammunition dump dug in just outside the village. A quick charge destroyed these. But they were obviously not having any impact on Tailleville itself. Finally Christian returned to Daughney. They decided to look for some kind of entrance. Soon the two officers saw a group of French inhabitants huddled below a large, solid wooden gate, the entrance to the château's courtyard. Christian ordered his driver to advance, and they battered open the gate and entered.

'C' Company poured in behind the tankers. The North Shores soon realized that Tailleville was no sleepy farm village. It had been turned into a German headquarters. Facilities were cleverly hidden underground. First-aid posts, garages, stables, barracks, munitions dumps and mess kitchens were all in an underground complex linked by tunnels. Other tunnels locked in with gun pits and firing trenches scattered throughout Tailleville.

Virtually every approach from one street to another was covered by at least one gun pit. Snipers ranged freely. They moved through the tunnels.

The North Shores tangled in a vicious battle. Every platoon was constantly exposed to rear attack by Germans using the tunnels. Slowly resistance was eliminated. But it took a painfully long time. For every German that surrendered, two fought to the death. Finally, the remaining Germans tried to escape into a nearby wood. The North Shores quickly blocked this escape route. About sixty Germans surrendered. Tailleville was taken. It was 2000 hours. Daylight was fading fast. The fight had raged for six hours.

The North Shores were to have advanced much farther on June 6. Now they were ordered to stand fast. They had paid a high price for the ground won. Of about 800 men, 125 had fallen. Thirty-four were dead.

The survivors were surprised to be alive and unhurt. Private Ian McFarlane was typical. Coming off the LCA that morning, Private Donald Young had been shot in the shoulder beside him. He was running for the seawall when his corporal had been shot down at his side. On the road to Tailleville, a shell landed on McFarlane's section and killed Private Earl Roderick Palmer and Corporal Fred Fraser. Then Platoon Sergeant William Girvan was wounded. In the melee in the village, Private C.W. McLaughlin was shot through the spine and left a paraplegic at age twenty-two. McFarlane had then made four terrifying forays into the underground warrens and fought wild firefights in narrow rooms and night-black passageways. He had lived through all this. But he could not stop thinking of the chums who had fallen. Mere chance seemed to determine who lived, who was maimed, who died.

CHAPTER FOURTEEN

The Canadian advance out of Bernières remained bogged down into the afternoon. Le Régiment de la Chaudière no sooner eliminated one machine-gun position than it came under fire from another. Gains were measured in yards.

Behind 8th Canadian Infantry Brigade's column, the battalions of 9th Brigade streamed ashore. Men and equipment packed the beach—a beach greatly shrunk by high tide. It was only about twenty-five yards wide when the Highland Light Infantry landed. Each man carried a collapsible bicycle on his shoulder.

They were to have saddled up and merrily pedaled to Carpiquet Airport. Instead, they faced a section of promenade so heavily wired there were only a couple of exit points. The beach, wrote their war diarist, was "jammed with troops with bicycles, vehicles and tanks all trying to move toward the exits. Movement was frequently brought to a standstill when a vehicle up ahead became stuck. It was an awful shambles and not at all like the organized rehearsals...More than one uttered a fervent prayer of thanksgiving that our air umbrella was so strong. One gun ranged on the beach would have done untold damage but the 9th CIB landed without a shot fired on them."

Bicycles still shouldered, the HLI finally entered Bernières. Many side streets were blocked by rubble from damaged or destroyed houses. Near the church, they could go no farther as the roads were blocked by the transport of the assaulting battalions. Everyone piled up behind, choking the roads, while the enemy positions up ahead were cleared.

HLI commander Lieutenant Colonel Frank Griffiths finally gave up. He gathered the battalion in the grounds of an estate next to the church.

"Here, we had a chance to drink a can of self-heating soup or cocoa and eat some bully beef and hard tack. Here the sun broke through and the day became quite hot and sultry," the war diarist noted.

While the HLI relaxed, Major General Rod Keller stormed about angrily. He had waded ashore minutes after the HLI. Wearing a beret, and with binoculars slung around his neck, the tall general was a commanding presence. After a few minutes posing for news cameramen, Keller demanded to know what was delaying the advance. He was told that the Chauds now not only faced machine guns, but were also being fired on by an 88-millimeter gun. This gun was literally sniping at anybody who moved. It was heavily protected by infantry in a trench.

Closest to the gun was Lieutenant Walter Moisan's No. 8 Platoon. He ordered an attack. The lead section under Corporal Bruno Vennes got within two hundred yards of the gun before being pinned down by heavy fire. Moisan led the soldiers in a low crawl to a thicket of brush. The brush was only thirty yards from the gun. Just as the Chauds were about to kill the gun crew with rifle fire, a bullet struck a phosphorous grenade on Moisan's web belt. The phosphorous set his clothing aflame and burned deeply into his flesh. Despite agonizing injuries, Moisan ordered Vennes to take out the gun before giving him any first aid.

Vennes led a mad dash into the trench system. His men locked in a wild melee with the Germans. Seeing his chance, Vennes ducked out of the trench and charged the gun. As he ran, Vennes chucked grenades at its crew.

All were killed by the explosions. Vennes then went back and helped win the trench. Returning to Moisan, he gave the badly injured lieutenant first aid until stretcher-bearers evacuated him to the beach. Moisan received a Military Cross and Vennes a Military Medal for their parts in this action.

* * *

Silencing the gun broke German resistance in the immediate area. The long snaking line of Canadians started again toward Bény-sur-Mer. Fort Garry Horse Shermans from 'A' Squadron were on point. The Chauds followed close behind. Then came the tanks of 'B' Squadron. The Queen's Own Rifles were at the rear.

All went well until the tanks butted up against snipers and machine-gun positions in front of Bény. The Chauds swung Major George Sévigny's 'C' Company out to screen the tanks.

A hot fight ensued that brought the column to another standstill.

Everything was taking too long. The Queen's Own were grousing that the Chauds were just dicking about. Fort Garry commander Lieutenant Colonel Ronald Morton agreed. The plan called for 8th Brigade to win the Anguerny ridgeline. This was still a good three miles from Bény. Once the ridge fell, 9th Brigade would pass through. Accompanied by the Sherbrooke Fusiliers tanks, the fresh brigade would dash the remaining five miles to Carpiquet Airport. But the afternoon was trailing away.

Bény finally fell to Sévigny's men. Then they headed for Basly, a mile beyond. The advance again tripped sniper and machine-gun opposition. The Chauds could only slowly, cautiously close on each German pocket. Sévigny was right up front, ensuring his men were aggressive. But killing or forcing the surrender of each point of resistance took time. Little could be done to speed things up.

The remaining Chauds were strung out on the road behind. Because of the thick hedgerows, they could not spread into adjacent fields and work around the German resistance. A Forward Observation Officer, Lieutenant J.B. Leslie, from 14th Field Regiment was on hand. Normally he would call artillery fire down on the Germans. But their positions were only revealed when the Chauds practically stepped on them. So Leslie was unable to shell them for fear of hitting Canadians.

Behind 8th Brigade, 9th Brigade shuffled off the beach. Obviously there was not going to be any fast dash. Most bicycles were ditched on the beach. Not until 1645 hours did the North Nova Scotia Highlanders reach Bény. They were supposed to reorganize for the dash to Carpiquet. The Sherbrookes were close by, getting rid of the various waterproofing devices on the tanks. These had taken two weeks to install. Plugging a strand of electrical wire into a live socket ignited explosive charges that blew the inflatable canvas screens off in seconds.

Once the Sherbrookes finished, the North Novas jumped on the tanks to race through to Carpiquet. But mortar fire dogged the advance from a ridge west of Bény. Sherbrooke commander Lieutenant Colonel Mel Gordon ordered 'A' Squadron to send a tank troop to destroy the mortars. Lieutenant Jack Casey's No. 1 Troop headed out.

Inside Casey's tank, a horrific image kept playing out in driver Richard Bryant's mind. When the tank had come ashore, the corporal had seen several Canadian corpses lying on the edge of the beach. Their clothes had been blown off by the force of an explosion caused when one had stepped on an anti-tank mine.

If I don't forget this, I'm not going to get through, Bryant kept thinking.

The three tanks quickly closed on the mortars. They were dug into a system of trenches. Poking his head and shoulders out of the turret hatch, Casey chucked grenades into the trench. When that failed to stop the mortar fire, the lieutenant ordered Bryant to drive closer. He wanted to cast grenades directly at the mortar crews.

"Sir, you're going to get your head blown off if you're not careful," Bryant warned.

Casey insisted. The grenades still didn't do the trick. To get a bigger bang, Casey wrapped a grenade and anti-personnel mine together. He threw several of these into the trench, killing a good number of Germans. As Casey got ready to throw another of his improvised charges, a machine-gun burst wounded him horribly in the head. Bryant spun the tank around and raced to a Regimental Aid Post. Casey died of his wounds on June 18.

When Casey was wounded, Sergeant R.R. Beardsley took over No. 1 Troop. The two remaining tanks stumbled upon a well-hidden battery of four 122-millimeter guns. These were protected by several machine guns and light anti-tank guns. The two Shermans were badly outgunned. But Beardsley silenced the position with a rapid flurry of accurate 75-millimeter rounds. Having eliminated the mortars and guns, the two tanks rejoined the main column.

* * *

The slow advance continued. Desperate to speed things up, Major Sévigny had cobbled together a mobile force. He mounted Lieutenant Willy Foy's No. 14 Platoon onto a troop of Fort Garry's 'A' Squadron tanks. The Chauds' Bren-carrier platoon under Captain Michel Gauvin was also brought forward. Sévigny jumped onto a tank and ordered it to lead the mobile force forward. They were to punch forward a mile from Basly to La Mare. "Stop for nothing," Sévigny said.

German snipers and machine guns fired repeatedly. But Sévigny ordered the Chauds to stay mounted. Tanks and carriers roared through without slowing. La Mare was quickly reached. Only twenty soldiers manning an anti-aircraft gun were there. They immediately surrendered. Sévigny ordered the column on to Colomby-sur-Theon, about a half mile beyond.

Colomby was surrounded by a high, stout stone wall. The village was also heavily defended. It took over an hour to clear. At about 1530 hours, Sévigny reported that the way was now open for 9th Brigade to pass through and advance on Carpiquet.

* * *

At Basly, the Queen's Own Rifles had broken from the column. They hooked to the left in order to seize the village of Anguerny. The Queen's Own soldiers had thought the Chauds overly timid. Now they realized this was wrong. Snipers constantly harassed them. Stubborn machine-gun positions appeared one after the other. Artillery and mortar fire was constant.

Company Sergeant Major Charlie Martin thought the advance inland "worse than the beach itself." They always advanced up an incline that enabled the Germans to see their every move. Whenever a machine gun opened up, the nearest platoon took to the fields, picking out draws, sloughs and low ground when they could. They needed to locate the enemy's machine-gun fire in order to pinpoint their own fire, and this was done in erratic bursts of running and flopping, stops and starts. It was exhausting and dangerous work. Martin was pained to see 'A' Company losing more men. Having lost so many on the beach, it didn't seem right.

Finally, at 1730 hours, they entered Anguerny. It consisted of ninety houses and about 240 people. A soldier who spoke a little French walked into Roger Chevalier's farmyard. He handed an orange to the farmer's two-year-old daughter. Thinking it was just a colorful ball, she started tossing the orange around. Since the Germans had come, the only fruit seen was what grew locally.

Chevalier was having trouble focusing. Out in the road lay the body of a Canadian killed by a German sniper. Chevalier watched in horror as Fort Garry tanks ground one after the other over the corpse. The tracks scattered the man's "guts all over the road." It was the cruelest thing Chevalier had ever seen. But when he pointed this out to the soldier, the man shrugged as if such a thing was routine.

When the Queen's Own finished securing Anguerny and nearby Anisy, the Fort Garry Horse were ordered back to Bény for the night. They were to regroup and reload with fuel and ammunition. In the morning, they would rejoin 8th Brigade and renew the advance.

* * *

It was about 2000 hours by the time 8th Brigade won all its objectives. This cleared the way for the North Novas and the Sherbrooke tankers to advance toward Carpiquet Airport. En route they were to capture Colomby-sur-Thaon and cut the Caen-Bayeux highway. It would be dark in about two hours. But 9th Brigade's Brigadier Ben Cunningham was optimistic they could cover the five miles to Carpiquet before last light. The infantry would ride on the tanks or in Bren carriers. The mechanized force was going for broke.

Cunningham unleashed a formidable force. Out front were the light Stuart tanks of the Sherbrookes' reconnaissance troop. Right behind were the North Novas' carrier platoon and 'C' Company riding in eighteen carriers. This infantry was followed by No. 11 Platoon of the Cameron Highlanders of Ottawa (MG). The Camerons had Vickers heavy machine guns loaded on carriers. They were trailed by a troop of M10 tank destroyers, two assault sections of the North Nova pioneer platoon, one section of its mortar platoon, and four of the battalion's anti-tank guns.

This leading element formed the tip of an arrowhead formation. On the right flank, 'A' Company was aboard the tanks of the Sherbrooke 'A' Squadron. The left flank was covered by 'B' Company on 'B' Squadron's Shermans. Bringing up the rear and traveling in the center, 'D' Company rode on 'C' Squadron. Lieutenant Colonel Don Petch had his headquarters in the middle of the column.

"Everyone was feeling keen," noted the North Novas' regimental historian. It was "as if they were on a new sort of scheme that played for keeps, but was exciting and not too dangerous. They knew the main objective was Carpiquet Airport and did not think there would be much trouble getting there."

For the first mile and a half it was a happy romp. Only wildly inaccurate snipers fired.

These were left to 'D' Company to clean up. Then the reconnaissance troop took a wrong turn and headed north toward Caen. 'C' Company began to follow before its commander realized the mistake and managed to get the force headed in the right direction.

Night was falling fast. The battle group was still four miles from Carpiquet Airport. There was no chance of reaching it before darkness set in. Realizing the force was highly vulnerable to being cut off from the rest of the Canadian division, Major General Keller ordered a halt. The battle group was to form a fortress where it was. The advance would be renewed in the morning.

CHAPTER FIFTEEN

Right of the main column, 7th Brigade's Royal Winnipegs had easily taken Creully by mid-afternoon. They were supported by Lieutenant Bill McCormick's No. 2 Troop from the 1st Hussars' 'C' Squadron. Leaving Creully, the force marched toward a large quarry that was the Winnipegs' final objective. McCormick hated doddering along beside the infantry. *Keep moving at this speed and you're a dead duck,* he thought. Finally McCormick ordered the tankers to move out alone. No. 2 Troop rolled. McCormick led with Corporal Jackie Simmons and Corporal Bill Talbot following.

Fifteen men in three tanks then carried out a remarkable run almost to Carpiquet Airport. They drove straight up the Caen-Bayeux highway. The only Germans met were scattered groups of infantry, who, McCormick later wrote, "either came out and surrendered or tried to crawl away through the wheat. As a tank troop we could not handle prisoners, so we disarmed them and sent them back down the road [toward Creully]. The rest we pursued with machine-gun fire and shell fire and continued on our way."

McCormick was increasingly sure nothing stood between his tanks and the airport. He stopped having the driver slow as they roared through one little hamlet after another.

Coming out of Camilly, McCormick saw a German scout car driving straight at his tank. As the scout car's driver swerved to pass, Trooper O.K. Hunter raked it with machine-gun fire. A second later, Trooper Gord Perkins swung the tank head-on into the car and crushed it against a stone wall. The car exploded into flames. The car's driver pitched forward to lie draped over the windshield. A passenger at his side was flung, burning, into the road.

The tankers raced on another mile without seeing a German. McCormick called a short halt for a rest. The lieutenant believed No. 2 Troop could easily reach Carpiquet Airport. He kept trying to raise 'C' Squadron on the radio. "Come up, come up," he pleaded. But there was only static.

A mile farther, McCormick paused again. He was outside a village called la Villeneuve. The airport was about two miles away. But McCormick knew the joyride was over. He could probably get to the airport. But his tanks were low on fuel and ammunition. They could never hold off an attack. McCormick ordered the Shermans turned about.

As No. 2 Troop passed through Camilly it was met by an astonished Canadian Scottish company commander. Major Arthur Plows was preparing to attack the village with 'A' Company when the tanks approached from the wrong direction. McCormick told Plows that Camilly was undefended. Plows already had his men formed for an attack. He was determined to go in that way. McCormick positioned his tanks to provide fire support. 'A' Company advanced across a field. An old lady sitting on a stool in the middle of it milked a cow. "[She] never even looked up as this battalion of infantry and tanks went by," McCormick said. "We just walked into the village. There was nothing there."

McCormick left the Can Scots to their village. He could still picture the airport in his mind, ripe for the taking. The lieutenant worried that by morning the Germans would pull themselves together and be ready to fight to stop the Canadian advance. Mostly, however, he just wanted to sleep. Like everyone else in the Allied invasion force, he was dead tired from an incredibly long day of almost constant battle.

CHAPTER SIXTEEN

McCormick's bold dash was the deepest penetration into Normandy achieved by any Allied force on D-Day. His tanks had gone nine miles as the crow flies, twelve miles via the route actually taken.

More important, the Canadians had advanced farther from the shore than anybody else. No American or British divisions came close to winning as much ground as 3rd Canadian Infantry Division. Having landed last, they had pushed up to six miles inland. Juno Beach was the second-most-hotly contested on D-Day. Only the Americans at Omaha Beach faced a stiffer fight, their advance facing dogged resistance almost every step of the way. The Canadians achieved a stunning feat of arms for which the soldiers of 3rd Division and 2nd Armored Brigade could be proud.

The cost in blood was high. At day's end, 340 Canadians were dead. Another 574 were wounded. Twenty-six subsequently died from wounds, bringing the death tally to 366. In addition to the Canadians killed or wounded, 243 British soldiers serving in various support roles also fell on Juno. But by day's end, 14,500 Canadians were ashore. They were part of a staggering invasion force. Almost 133,000 soldiers were ashore by nightfall.

* * *

Out on the front lines, emotions numbed by the horror of combat began to be felt. Major Elliott Dalton sat alone. His brother, Charles, had been left on the beach. The head wound Charles had suffered as he led his company onto the sand had been serious. He had been evacuated to a hospital ship. And now word was that he had died. Elliott believed it was true. No way could both have led the Queen's Own Rifles' assault wave and neither die.

Aboard the hospital ship, meanwhile, Charles lay on a cot. His head was swathed in bandages. He suffered from severe concussion. But Charles cared not about his condition. He suffered from awful news. News that Elliott had been killed just a short distance inland.

It would be weeks before either brother knew the reports of their sibling's death were false.

Back at Elliott's 'A' Company, Company Sergeant Major Charlie Martin walked the lines. Suddenly he saw a match flare. Somebody lit a cigarette. Martin shouted at the man to douse it. Was he trying to draw sniper fire? From the man's shape, Martin realized he had just dressed down Lieutenant Colonel Jock Spragge. He didn't care. Instead, Martin strode over and gave him hell. Martin told him he should be back at Battalion HQ, not up front with them—the last line between our forces and the enemy. "He was too good and too necessary to be killed or wounded. He gave me one of those looks that anyone who ever knew Jock Spragge would recognize and said, 'Charlie, it's such a sad day. We've lost so many good men.' He said goodnight and turned away, but not before I saw the tears in his eyes."

Martin walked back to 'A' Company with some heavy thoughts about the Colonel's burden and about the Queen's Own Rifles of Canada, 8th Brigade, 3rd Division, and their landing in Normandy that day. "That any of us had survived seemed like a miracle."

It was a miracle. And also the end of the most critical day of World War II. The Canadian success at Juno Beach—along with the British and American successes at the other beaches— established an Allied toehold on continental Europe. A toehold from which they would soon begin the long, hard march leading ultimately to Germany, victory and the end of the most terrible war in human history.

INDEX

Assault on Juno is **MARK ZUEHLKE**'s second book in the Rapid Reads series. *Ortona Street Fight* documented Canada's first major triumph of World War II—the December 1943 battle for Ortona, Italy. With more than twenty books to his credit, Zuehlke has been hailed as Canada's leading popular military historian. He is also an award-winning mystery writer. Mark lives in Victoria, British Columbia.

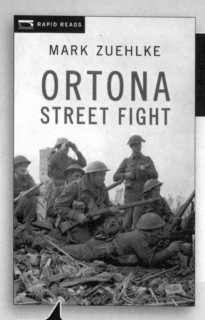

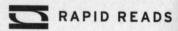